MW00380789

FOR LOVE OF ORCAS
AN ANTHOLOGY

Edited by
Andrew Shattuck McBride
and Jill McCabe Johnson

Jill McCabe Johnson

Wandering Aengus Press
Eastsound, WA

Library of Congress Cataloguing-in-Publication Data available.

ISBN: 978-0-578-46277-6

Cover image taken by John Durban, Ph.D., and Holly Fearnbach, Ph.D. from an unmanned octocopter at >100ft using non-invasive, aerial photogrammetry during a research collaboration between National Oceanic and Atmospheric Administration's Southwest Fisheries Science Center, Sealife Response + Rehab + Research (SR3) and the Coastal Ocean Research Institute. Research authorized by NMFS permit #19091.

 Wandering Aengus Press
PO Box 334 Eastsound, WA 98245

Printed in the United States of America.

Sam Hamill's "The End of the Road from Nantucket" from *Habitation* (Lost Horse, 2014) is published with permission from the Sam Hamill Literary Estate, Paul E. Nelson, Literary Executor.
Excerpt from *Blonde Indian* by Ernestine Saankaláxt Hayes. © 2006 The Arizona Board of Regents. Reprinted by permission of the University of Arizona Press.
Eva Saulitis' excerpts from *Leaving Resurrection: Chronicles of a Whale Scientist* (Boreal Books, 2008) are published with permission from the Eva Saulitis Literary Estate, Peggy Shumaker, Literary Executor.
Robert Sund's "In America" and "Salmon Moon" from *Poems From Ish River Country* (Shoemaker & Hoard, 2004) are published with permission from the Robert Sund Poet's House, Tim McNulty, Literary Executor.

This work is informed, in part, by support from the National Endowment for the Humanities for participation in the 2018 Summer Institute, The Native American West: A Case Study of the Columbia Plateau. Any views, findings, conclusions, or recommendations expressed in this publication do not necessarily reflect those of the National Endowment for the Humanities.

CONTENTS

Editors' Notes

I watched videos of Tahlequah (J35) carrying her dead calf, and followed the news of her 17-day, 1000-mile journey, and found a new kind of grief. I worried about Tahlequah. I read Paul E. Nelson's "Elegy for Tahlequah's Calf" in *Cascadia Magazine*, and Craig van Rooyen's "How to Swim an Elegy" in *Rattle*.

On August 8, 2018 my poet friend Jill McCabe Johnson and I were messaging on Twitter about Tahlequah and her calf. We admired the two poems by Nelson and van Rooyen.

Privately, I wondered if poets, writers and artists might help save the Southern Resident orcas. I asked Jill, "Do you think there might be interest in an anthology ... in response to the plight of the Southern Resident orcas?" Jill replied, "I love this idea. Are you thinking of editing this?" I answered, "Possibly." Jill added, "We have to make this happen!" And so we started our work.

Our sense of urgency increased as we learned that Scarlet (J50) was ailing and then presumed dead.

I am grateful to Jill McCabe Johnson for her response, for her offer of Wandering Aengus Press as a home for this anthology, for her gorgeous cover and for all of her work. I am grateful, too, to all of the poets, writers, and artists who encouraged us and submitted work for this anthology. It was challenging to choose from so much beautiful, heartfelt work.

I thank Joseph K. Gaydos of the SeaDoc Society for his work and for his contribution to *For Love of Orcas*. There are many other people and organizations working on behalf of the Southern Resident orcas, Chinook salmon, and their ecosystem. Their ecosystem is ours; these efforts deserve our participation and financial support.

Andrew Shattuck McBride

The poet's job has always been to celebrate what's plum in the world and oppose what is not, to bring light to the disheartened, give voice to the downtrodden, and revel when beauty and balance prevail. In the last one hundred years, the Southern Resident orca population has gone from thriving to critically endangered, just as their main food source, the Chinook salmon, has become endangered. The imbalance in their populations and for many other endangered species is a direct result of the imbalance in how we live our lives.

The Coastal and Inland Salish, who for millennia have fished for salmon to feed their people, have a saying, "Take only what you need." If we fail to heed this advice, we will plunder and deplete our natural resources to the point where we take not only from the planet and each other today, but for all future generations. Reversing the damage we've already caused will take fast action and, yes, changes to how we live now. Fortunately, some of those changes can have relatively quick effects, such as removing obsolete and inefficient dams. Others can even benefit human health directly, such as switching to plant-based plastics in our food supply and waste stream.

This book is not a how-to for saving the planet. Instead, it's a reminder of the complex and exquisite beauty surrounding us. Our hope is that readers will care enough to coalesce and bring our interactions with and effects on that beauty back into balance. Plus, proceeds from sales of the book will benefit the SeaDoc Society's efforts to restore the Southern Resident orcas and their extended ecosystem.

Thank you to the authors and artists who sent us their moving works, to SeaDoc and all the organizations and individuals working to save Southern Resident orcas, and especially to my visionary co-editor, Andrew Shattuck McBride, whose brainchild this anthology is. Working with him on this book has been a privilege.

Jill McCabe Johnson

SAVING SOUTHERN RESIDENT KILLER WHALES

Killer whales, also known as orca, a diminutive of their Latin name *Orcinus orca*, are a cosmopolitan species. Even though they can be found in all of the world's oceans, over the last 250,000 years sub-populations have been diverging as they pass cultural knowledge along from one generation to the next. In many places they now exist as discrete ecotypes that can be genetically distinct, physically different and have unique languages and specialized diets. Such populations can even overlap, but not interact. For example, within the Salish Sea there are two groups of fish-eating killer whales that specialize in eating Chinook salmon (northern and southern residents), a population that only eats marine mammals (transients), and another fish-eating group called offshores that specializes in eating sharks.

Southern Resident orca are icons of the Pacific Northwest. Scientists call them "flagship" conservation species. Rally the public to save them and you will save the ecosystem. Each animal can be uniquely identified by their dorsal fin and saddle patch and are given not only alphanumeric identifications but also names. They are friends to the people who live here and in them we see reflections of our aspirations and ourselves.

For example, last summer J35, a 20-year-old orca known as Tahlequah, gave birth to a girl only to have her die just a short time later. For the next 17 days, people around the world watched as this mother carried her baby with her for over a thousand miles. Mourning behavior has been noted in other long-lived highly social animals including primates and several species of toothed whales related to orcas. As the public grieved along with Tahlequah they also demanded that action be taken to improve environmental conditions for this small population of killer whales that, as of this writing, number only 75, likely half the size that the population used to be prior to western settlement in the region.

The citizens of the Salish Sea are faced with a decision: dramatically change how we think about and invest in ecosystem restoration or risk losing Southern Resident killer whales forever. For over 200 years we have been altering the rivers and estuaries needed by Chinook salmon to survive. Dams block the passage of young smolts heading to the ocean and adult salmon returning to the rivers to spawn. We have over-harvested fish leaving insufficient animals to reproduce and create the next generation. And now, the carbon we have been putting into the atmosphere is not only warming, but also acidifying the ocean.

Our scientific understanding of the Salish Sea and how it works tells us that we are long past the point of band-aid measures like only increasing hatchery salmon or culling seals and sea lions who also eat Chinook salmon. Now is the time to maximize efforts to restore rivers and shorelines that support the food and habitat salmon need so they can flourish and provide the orca with enough to eat. Dams like the four on the Lower Snake River should be breached. We must also reduce ocean noise that pervades the orcas' feeding areas and disrupts communication and finding food by echolocation, and clean up the persistent toxic chemicals that we dumped in the ocean and now contaminate and suppress the immune systems of the whales we profess to love.

The lives of salmon, orca, and people are inextricably linked. Full-scale ecosystem restoration will save salmon, orcas, and us. It is time to go all out and take care of this place as if our lives and our livelihoods depend on it. Because they do.

Joseph K. Gaydos

FOR LOVE OF ORCAS

ELEGY FOR TAHLEQUAH'S CALF

For David McCloskey

Tahlequah is daughter of Princess Angeline
brother of Moby, sister to Kiki, mother
to Notch. Her second offspring was not
born but born still and still un-named &
un-numbered. For five days Tahlequah

.

pushed her still-born calf around the
Salish Sea, perhaps a hope that she'd
not be a parent to bury a child, perhaps
a grief vigil, the un-named/un-numbered
calf riding dead on her rostrum five days.

.

Tahlequah, Cherokee for "plains" or a kind
of red rice, or "just two" or "two is enough."
Or a ferry terminal on Vashon. Five days
says the witness from the whale museum
sitting shiva and watching her "deep breaths."

.

She carried the dead calf 20 miles one day
in her teeth from time to time through the
full Ripe Thimbleberry Moon, through stage
one grief, denial. "We are going to be here
as long as necessary for her." Here

.

is what your ferry-line idling of your
giant truck brings, 108.7 degree low
temperatures in Quriyat, Oman, eleven
fires in the Arctic Circle, momma whales
pushing around their still-born calves five days.

.

3

But you stayed cool in your air-conditioned
life, you had bigger fish to fry than whales
who have no lobby, you idled that engine
until the last glacier died, the last salmon
leapt & last forest burned.

.

These are the stories the children of our
children will tell if there are storytellers
in their time. How we slept at the switch
ignored the clear signs of doom, how we
were scholars of war & good tweeters

.

had nice dinner photographs & saved ourselves
from Muslims & immigrants & every vague
threat the cruel majority could conjure
while the world burned & one whale mom
did all our crying for us.

Paul E. Nelson

A Fractured Cycle

Your ancestors, deemed sacred by the Chinook,
followed an ancient cycle of river and sea,
aging in a boundless ocean before discarding
blue cloaks and assuming the blush
of mating season. Their final act:
to spawn in fresh water.

Now you emerge from an egg your mother buried
among riverbed gravel. As you grow you avoid
the angler's hook, evade man-made dams.
You survive contaminants ushered in by floods.

Reaching the ocean that once welcomed your kind,
you are embraced by arms far too warm. An acidic
tongue laps your skin while you struggle to fatten
for the journey back to the river that birthed you.

M. Stone

WORDS OF ENCOURAGEMENT

One must always pretend something
Among the dying

—W.S. Merwin

When writing poems about extinction
it's important that you make the poems
deep, but uplifting.

Nobody wants to read a bummer poem
about endangered orcas and their dead babies.
Keep it light. Keep it motivational. Encouraging.

It's important to accommodate your gentle reader.
Don't say anything about how "If you won't
swim in it, why should they have to live in it?"

Don't say that. Honesty is offensive
in this day and age. It's always been offensive.
How else do you suppose we got here?

Maybe, instead of saying something like,
"The orcas and salmon are going extinct
because of ordinary greed and apathy,"

instead, say something like, "The noble creature
with his power and grace, shall journey away
forever, through the portals of time."

Good taste, omits mention of ~
(baby orcas, abducted to be theme park clowns—
decades in chlorinated cages, taking their eyes—

how during the capture, so many died.)
Don't forget, to forget what you know
about human cruelty—

how the baby orcas that didn't survive
had their bellies slit and filled with stones,
then were sewn closed

and dumped into the sea,
to sink into a silence so dark and so deep
public outrage couldn't reach—

a depth unfathomable as a mother's grief—
too heavy to carry for one day, much less 17.
Among the dying, shall we pretend

that in the end, we too, shall not be listed
among the dead? Yes. Let's pretend,
when writing poems about extinction.

Rena Priest

ORCAS IN THE MIST

The little orca surfaces under an Apocalyptic red sun barely visible behind a shroud of smoke from the wildfires burning across the West.

We're headed east down the Strait of Juan de Fuca toward Washington's San Juan Island, pacing a three-year-old killer whale named Scarlet, also known as J50, as she travels with her mother, brother, and older sister in endless pursuit of salmon.

All four whales are part of J Pod, now known around the world for the display of grief by pod member J35, or Tahlequah, who carried her dead newborn for 17 days and 1,000 miles. It was a protest march against all that we've done to kill off these magnificent animals by starving them of their food source, poisoning their water and prey, and filling their habitat with incessant vessel traffic.

I'm here as a volunteer along with a team of whale specialists and a wildlife veterinarian under federal permit to assess and document Scarlet's health. As she rises for a gulp of the same smoky air we're breathing, her short, sharp blow is met with groans aboard our small boat. None of us have ever seen such a skinny whale.

For those of us who live among the orcas, Scarlet meant hope. She was a Christmas present, born at the end of December 2014 in the main fjord of the small island I live on, called, coincidentally, Orcas.

There's an informal West Coast cult of the killer whale that's devoted to J, K, and L Pods, which together make up the Southern Resident killer whales who spend a good part of their year foraging and socializing in the Washington State and British Columbian inland waters that make up the Salish Sea. In 50 years, this clan of supersize dolphins has gone from being vilified and shot by fishermen to being rounded up for marine parks—48 Southern Residents were caught or killed during the capture operations in the sixties and seventies—to becoming the most iconic creature of the Pacific Northwest wilds.

Those wilds are myth now. Ecosystem disruption reaches every part of the region. Climate change is exacerbating wildfires, killing seabirds, and melting the Cascades snowpack earlier—making the streams less suitable for salmon. Our centuries of assault on the rivers, forests, estuaries, and coastlines have done a number on this remarkable place.

And the numbers are looking very bad for killer whales, the apex predator in a dysfunctional environment. After the captures stopped, the Southern Resident population climbed from 70 to a high of 98 in 1995. Then they dropped again, to below 80, and were declared federally endangered by Canada in 2001 and by the United States in 2005. In 2015, they were named one of NOAA's Species in the Spotlight, the animals most at risk of extinction and deserving of extra effort and attention.

The Southern Residents numbered just 78, with no live births in more than two years, when Scarlet came along. Born to a beautiful female named Slick, Scarlet was the first of what became known as the baby boom, with eight calves added to J and L Pods over the following 13 months. A compact black-and-white package of pure exuberance, Scarlet represented everything we love about these playful, caring, intelligent, highly social animals, who stick together tighter than most human families.

Nearly all the wild orcas seen in the condition Scarlet's in have died, and Scarlet is a precious female, potentially producing up to six calves over her lifetime.

Whether she lives or dies, Scarlet's poor health and Tahlequa's grief are just two agonizing illustrations of a larger picture: that the current state of the Southern Resident killer whales is a disgrace and a huge embarrassment for the U.S. and Canada.

We've declared the orcas national and regional treasures, bestowed upon them our strongest protections, yet we continue to kill them with building permits, logging, ranching and farming leases, fishing quotas, and dam permits, which all affect the Chinook salmon that these orcas need to survive.

When we left Scarlet after following her that day on the water, she was chugging along at four knots. She hit a wall of current as the tide changed, and her family forged ahead in search of food, which orcas commonly share with their podmates. Scarlet fell a thousand yards behind the others but gamely continued pushing east. We lost sight of her small dorsal fin as the chop came up, her faint blows lost in the smoke from hundreds of fires.

Bob Friel

SALISH SEA ACCOUNT

account—noun. Report, story, log, tally, balance sheet, debt

2009, the year the U.S. Board on Geographic Names adopted the name Salish Sea to pay tribute to the first inhabitants of the region, the Coast Salish.

7,000 square miles—the total marine area of the Salish Sea. These inland waters include Washington State's Puget Sound, the Strait of Juan de Fuca, and the San Juan Islands.

8,000,000 people live and work beside the Salish Sea.

75 (as of this writing) Southern Resident Killer Whales (SRKWs or orcas) live in the Salish Sea, down from 86 when they were listed as endangered in 2005.

3 pods of SRKWs reside in the Salish Sea—J, K, and L Pods.

J35 (also known as Tahlequah) is a 20-year-old orca whose newborn calf survived for only 30 minutes on 7-24-18.

17, the number of days Tahlequah carried the 400-pound body of her dead calf through the sea.

1,000 miles, the distance Tahlequah traveled the Salish Sea with her pod while pushing her dead calf.

J50 (also known as Scarlet) died, 9-13-18. The 3-year-old female began losing weight in 2017.

30 Chinook/King salmon are typical in an orca's daily diet.

15 major dams built on the Snake River since the 1890s.

130,000 adult salmon and steelhead returned to the Snake River to spawn in the 1950s; in 2017, under 10,000.

3,600,000,000 dollars (U.S.) spent by the Canadian government to buy Kinder Morgan's Trans Mountain pipeline and expand transport of tar sands oil from Alberta, Canada to refineries in Northwest Washington and then ship elsewhere on the Salish Sea.

on account of—owing to, due to, as a consequence of

3 main threats to SRKWs: insufficient salmon, toxic water, noise pollution.

4 dams on the Lower Snake River impede migration to breeding habitat for Chinook salmon.

7 times more oil tankers (each holding 25,000,000 gallons of tar sands oil mixed with volatile organic diluents, including benzene) will travel the Salish Sea if the Trans Mountain pipeline expands.

0% chance to clean up tar sands oil (diluted bitumen or "dil bit") and protect first responders and marine life from toxic chemicals when tankers spill.

96 commercial whale-watching boats operated in the Salish Sea in 2015, up from 63 in 1999.

500,000 people annually watch whales on charters or private boats.

accountable—adjective. Responsible, liable, comprehensible, understandable

50 percent reduction in acoustic disturbance and a 15 percent increase in Chinook/King salmon would achieve the 2.3% annual SRKW growth needed to assure survival.

$40,000,000 – 50,000,000 was generated by the whale watching industry in 2015 (San Juan Tourism Bureau). No accounting of whether education and appreciation of whales due to watching outweigh the disruption of whales' feeding and breeding.

17 minutes of silence observed at vigils following the death of Tahlequah's calf.

1 Canadian Federal Court of Appeal overturned approval of the Trans Mountain oil pipeline expansion because the federal government failed to adequately consult First Nations.

44 state, tribal, provincial and federal officials serve on the Southern Resident Orca Task Force and will recommend solutions to the Washington governor and legislature.

Countless, the achievable solutions to pay our overdue debt to orcas and the Salish Sea.

Iris Graville

HALFWAY DOWN AN ALDER SLOPE

But what surface have we fallen through,
Here beneath the trees? What do we see in our infinity
if each is all the same, or all unknown?

—Molly Lou Freeman

Halfway down an alder slope, through an opening in the jumble of branches and leaves, Craig's son Lars spots them. "Look, killer whales! They're coming into the bay!" Even though he's only eight, Lars knows whales from a mile away and five hundred feet up. Since he was six months old, he and his sisters have been bundled and stashed on his parents' research boats every summer. At Whale Camp, he rubbed holes in his baby socks bouncing on the wall tent's plywood floor, his Johnny Jump-Up suspended from the ridgepole. "Listen," he says, "you can even *hear* them. They're over *there*." He points; we squint. There, in ponds of sunlight, we see black fins, breath smoke.

"Good eyes, Lars," says Craig. "Let's go." We lurch down the mountainside, branches tearing at our hair and our faces.

On the beach, we gallop, digging wedges into the sand with our rubber boots. In the distance, a few yards offshore, the first bubble-cloud rises, and we run for it. A fin slits shadows at the sea edge. When we get closer, we tiptoe. Five killer whales slide along shore, releasing air so they can sink. White bubble-rings bloom and phosphoresce on the water's surface. It's called beach-rubbing. On beaches with particular slopes and small, round pebbles, killer whales approach shore to slide their bodies along the bottom. One bay to the south, in the winter of 1918-19, the artist Rockwell Kent, holed up with his nineteen-year-old son at the homestead of Lars Olson, a seventy-one-year-old Swede, observed the phenomenon. Kent might have seen the mother of Aialik, the oldest female in this group, rubbing on his beach.

Craig and I, unthinking, pull off our boots and socks, make to unbutton our shirts and jeans, to jump into the water, where the whales are. Lars asks, "What are you guys doing?" and we look at each other and laugh. What *are* we doing? We fall heavily onto the beach, side by side and watch. The fifty yards separating the whales from us might as well be the Gulf of

Alaska. We can't—and shouldn't—cross it.

Even though we've been studying killer whales for two decades, fishermen still don't quite understand what we do out here. They call us "whale watchers." They shake their heads at Craig, a fisherman himself for twenty years, who, instead of sleeping during closures, raced off in this seine skiff to find killer whales.

Listen, I want to say, we're not *tourists*. We're doing *research*.

But what we do *is* watch. We watch from shore, with our boots askew on the ground. We watch from the boat's deck, poised with our notebooks, pencils, cameras, binoculars, with vials in which we place samples of whale skin. The whales visit our dreams, where they watch us. So what should we be called—scientists, voyeurs, observers, natural historians, writers, intruders, watchers? The killer whales are called *aaxlu*, *tukxukuak, agliuk, mesungesak, polossatik, skana, keet*, feared one, grampus, blackfish, orca, big-fin, fat-chopper. Whale killer. From the realm of the dead. *Orcinus orca*.

Eva Saulitis

J35 (TAHLEQUAH)

Somehow, we are amazed by grief—
        its spectacle. Spectre

of light off the water, endangered
        now. Her family surrounds her

as she pushes. As she lets her dead calf
        breach. As she swoops

at the last second. Before & again, rescue
        is retrieval. Yet, there,

next to her, the few orcas that remain,
        starve. For wild salmon.

For silence. For less of us, to watch.
        She pushes. She pushes through

water. She pushes through.
        And the world watches. Witness.

Her calf, still carried. So still. The heaviest
        grail. Something akin to grace.

Chelsea Dingman

IMAGES OF THE FUTURE MAY BE CLOSER THAN THEY APPEAR

Easy to call them whales,
these islands rising dark
from the darker sound,
distant bodies of stone
lifting as living creatures
while creatures living
below our visible
world rise, exhale spray
into the sky—whale weather.

Knowing they are under
where the ferry churns
across, I'll confess
I've never seen orcas
in the wild. Only penned.
When haze smudges
the islands, when smoke
blows down from the north, hangs
a gray screen, easy to wish

for rain to clean the air,
to rinse it—where?
Call it smoke weather,
call it acid rain,
call it into the ocean
the whales see dying.
Then what will wash up
on those beaches—what
will the tide bring when

it's black and white
in front of us, when we
are still not looking?

Joannie Stangeland

rumours of orcas—
a blood red moon
over the sound

Michael Dylan Welch

AND THEN THE SAILOR HEARS THE SEA

Only wind knows
        what water carries, as in

air you can't breathe.
        Sailor, you speak to me in hulls—

pounding, flowing, splitting. I end
somewhere, on all sides.

My blue talks abandoned languages
        subsumed by everything above.

You listen to wind pass
        against your ears, empty

like sea shells washed by every Caspian coast.
        What I am on my surface

draws you out. What I am
        inside is your lost ground.

One day you will return to water.

That day started when you discovered
        how to climb wind.

Nima Kian

HOW DEATH WORKS

The fruit is ripe for the taking
and we take. There is
no other wisdom.

—Marge Piercy
"September Afternoon at Four O'Clock"

they appear out of nowhere and clutch our hearts,
black and white leaping torpedoes of grace,
six-ton muscles of god, they are everything
we wish to be: powerful and free and otherworldly.
we forget they are just beautiful killers.

and tahlequah, seventeen days nosing
her limp calf, cold, rotting, through the salish sea.
make no mistake, there is a message.

look at my dead child.
look what you've done.

vision yourself an orca. pursued
by tourists every summer day.
inundated by boat noise and naval explosions.
poisoned by the runoff from millions of people—
their cars, dogs, lawns, toilets, industries.
starved by our salmon killing habits.
the fruit, we take it.

look at my dead child.
look what you've done.

let me ask you.
have you stopped eating cascadian chinook?
sold your boat? sold your car?
stopped flushing your toilet?
blown up a dam?
i thought not.
neither have i.
we have made our decision.
the fruit is ripe.

> *look at my dead child.*
> *look at what you've done.*

goodbye orcas.
fare thee well in the spirit world.
our temporary pleasure and comfort
is more important than your survival.
until the day we have to say

> *look at our dead child.*
> *look what we've done.*

look hard.
there is no other wisdom.
a piece of god is dead.
we will be next.

Luther Allen

CLAUDE LÉVI-STRAUSS PACES THE BEACH AT POINT WHITEHORN, WASHINGTON

*Mythical thought always progresses from the awareness
of oppositions to their resolution.*
—Claude Lévi-Strauss, *Structural Anthropology*

The ocean's voice silences all others—
hush, hush—speaking wind as its myth
of origin. Between waves, I hear

the phonemes *gneiss, schist, gneiss*:
the land and the Salish Sea exchanging
beach stones to enact their kinship.

But what mediating element resolves
the opposition between life and death?

I see trickster Raven everywhere,
shifting shapes, reconciling prey and predator,
scavenging both into himself.

And here, the ritual of salmon is casting a coho
awash on the shore. Already it has exchanged
its life for the lives of its daughters and sons.

It struggled from Cascade creek to river to ocean
and returned: the structure of every story
of going out and coming back.

I see death and life synthesize in the telling
of salmon swimming away and home,
of the ocean voicing, *forth, back, forth.*

Jennifer Bullis

In America

In America, the sea brings up rubber gloves,
orange spots in the pure sand.
And egg cartons and grapefruit and glass jars.
Mahogany two-by-fours.
Cedar poles from Japan, strips of bark
    still clinging to them.
Immense old cedar logs logged long ago.
Peeled fir. Old shoes.
Boom logs with rusty chain.
Wire cable spools.
Legs of tables. Pillows. Whiskey bottles.
Boxes with names in fading black paint.
Why say it anyway?
Light bulbs.
Butt ends of logs stamped with the codes
of Crown Zellerbach, Weyerhaeuser
and Georgia Pacific.
Vinegar bottles with Russian labels.
Nylon rope, blue, gaudy green, yellow and orange.
And garbage from fishermen,
    grapefruit halves mostly,
    and instant coffee jars
overboard at night,
washed up
        into this pure morning.

Robert Sund

COFFEE SHOP, WATERSHED, ORCA

This is not complicated.
It's just a poem about a coffee shop.

About some people, some cups,
some noise and newspapers, books

and laptops, puddles drying outside,
sun glinting off the windshield

of a seen-better-days Ford pickup.
The coffee tastes burnt. The headlines

scald my eyes. Whales and watershed
crowd my peripheral vision.

Exchanged words, clink
and murmur, cough and rasp of steam

in milk. Untasted for a thousand
miles by Tahlequah's calf. Not all

black and white, not the news,
not the pink-tongued whale

who does not say *watershed*
but comprehends a mountainside's

spawn in a shake of newspaper whose
front page carries another starving

orca as I sip my privileged cup,
boots recalling the faint hiss

of spongy moss, fizz of saturated
soil, leopard slugs, platter-size

maple leaves turning to lace.
This forest, this water, this noise,

this room not my own, I wobble
and dive, unbalanced by death,

pectoral fins flung to avoid a clatter
of cups, a hardpan slope burned

in the last conflagration, a scraping
hollowness in every misted blow.

Binary blur, zeroes and ones,
companioned by hunger, we do not touch,

absorbed in our serious division.
We cannot see our dreams.

We do not yet recognize
the sequence of our power.

J.I. Kleinberg

REQUIEM: OR *I WILL NOT YIELD*

1. *Orcinus orca* is a toothed whale belonging to the oceanic dolphin family. Apex predators, no animal but man preys on *Orca*.

We stood waist-deep in freezing water, our small bodies pulled deeper by the bump and sway of the waves
The sky was fog that bled into ocean, a study of grey on grey
Far off black shapes moved along the horizon
"Whales!!" our screams split the silence.

2. *Orcinus* means *of the kingdom of the dead* or *belonging to Orcus*. Orcus was a Roman god of the underworld, the punisher of broken promises.

In winters we spent hours racing through freezing waves, across cold, wet rocks
No words or books could hold us—the world was ours—and always
The hope of whales—*killer whales!* —moving in the hundreds just off-shore

3. We have caused the annihilation of eighty-three percent of all species. In 1954-1997 whalers killed over 5,000 Orca. In 1979-80 alone Soviet whalers killed more than 3,000.

One late summer we stood in sand warm and oozing over our toes
We watched, solemn silent children, as a group of men and women poured water
Over the body of a beached whale—we already knew s/he was dead

4. *Orca* are notable for their complex societal structures including matrilineal family groups known as pods—the most stable groups of any animal species.

My grandfather told me that whales were a nuisance—and *Orca* worst of all
Fishermen would shoot them to keep them from their catch
The sea, he said, *is full of them.*

5. *Orca* captured in Puget Sound in the 1970s had bullet scars. The U.S. Navy claimed to have deliberately killed hundreds in the 1950s with machine-guns, rockets, and depth charges.

How do we tell our stories when the oceans are empty
How do we sing our songs when the oceans are empty

6. They threw noisemakers into the water to drive pods of *Orca* into a narrow cove, blocked the way out, then pulled baby whales from the water. The Southern Resident community lost more than fifty family members to captivity.

Namu the Killer Whale arrived in Seattle in 1965
I *remember* him although that is not possible—he died in 1966—
Memory is like that—rewriting what we *want* to remember

Yvonne Garrett

IN SEARCH OF RESIDENTS

Telegraph Cove

Aside from being tired,
    I'm wet also. I'm storm surge
        and paddling. I'm in a family
of adventurers all who tend
    to watch this kind of stuff
        on TV. Somewhere in this
ocean, orcas. And somewhere
    in my mind, I expect a sort
        of miracle—orca breaching,
orca waltzing, orca sliding
    up to my kayak and offering
        me a mammal to mammal
high-five. We're three days in
    and we've seen a lot
        of birds. We're calling
out—*ORCA!* (log)
    ORCA! (dark spot on a wave).
        Maybe our desire to connect
is too much for this giant
    world. The orcas have no idea
        how much we watch for them,
or maybe they do, maybe
    they watch for us too.

Kelli Russell Agodon

TRIPLE ACROSTIC: ORCAS

Why the pods that used to streak and shimmy
     in Puget Sound's granitic light
have disappeared in recent decades: the reasons
     speed like a killer Chris Craft through clouded
inland waters. Reasons subtle as a buccaneer's
     logic: Goliath-girthed trunks of
Douglas fir that shadowed these estuaries
     and mussel-crowded coves—all felled
by axes that traveled ever farther up the temperate rainforest's
     northernmost reaches, their salal-shadowed mosses
exempted from protection by our bombast. In the global
     dance that warms to its own internal warnings, coastlines
yield like Roosevelt elk hides espaliered against a
       wall map of the illusory Northwest Passage—
     aquatinted waves where the shades of orcas frolic.

In memory of "K7," a.k.a. "Lummi,"
leader of the Puget Sound K Pod,
disappeared in December 2007
at about 98 years of age.

Carolyne Wright

From a Distance

From the ferry deck, John and I spot them, Southern Resident orcas shimmering like waves near Lopez Island. A few other passengers soon notice the black and white forms in the Salish Sea. Several boats appear around the whales, and what at first looks like one kayak turns to more, the combined vessels forming an entourage. A barometer of marine health in the Pacific Northwest, the popularity of these endangered whales soars even as their numbers decrease.

Our ferry threads between the San Juan Islands, leaving the whales behind in open water. The Southern Residents, numbering a new low, are threatened by several factors, noise and the presence of boat traffic among them. Marine traffic disturbs the vocalizations of the whales, compromising their ability to communicate.

Of more immediate concern, the proximity of boats, whether motorized or not, impacts the whales' feeding time, our hunger to experience the orcas contributing to their own. A 2017 annual report from the Soundwatch Boater Education Program reported an average of 12 boats observed within a half-mile of the whales throughout the summer months, traffic causing them to spend time traveling rather than foraging according to a Southern Resident Task Force Report.

The Pacific Whale Watching Association, an organization of whale-watching vessels, has adopted voluntary guidelines in addition to a federal and state law keeping vessels at a 200-yard distance from the whales. The group recommends reducing speeds within .65 miles of the whales and limiting time watching them, along with a no-go zone along the western shore of San Juan Island, a feeding spot for the whales. Lime Kiln Park on the island's western edge is, in fact, an excellent public place to view the whales from land, as breathtaking photos reveal.

Along with voluntary steps taken by businesses and individuals, the Southern Resident Task Force, a group of governmental and tribal agencies charged with a longer-term plan for the Southern Residents, has proposed recommendations with vessels in mind. Among them are doubling the distance of vessels to whales to 400 yards; creating a no-wake zone for commercial and pleasure boats; limiting the number of whale-watching craft at a time; and using fuel-efficient ferries resulting in less noise. A longer-term proposal even includes "quiet days" for the whales, with no vessels allowed to trail them.

On the ferry ride back from our weekend trip, I scour the water, combing waves for what might be another domino flash of a Southern Resident. I stare hard, old habits tough to break though I'm missing other sea life along the way, calling gulls and dark loons. No whales emerge on the outskirts of our return trip, not this time. Maybe they've found a discrete corner of the Salish Sea to feed in calmer waters. From a sun-warmed seat, Lopez Island comes and goes. Mount Baker disappears in the clouds, and I don't have to witness the whales firsthand to know they're home.

Gail Folkins

Surrounded by Freedom

The late sun reflects off the almost calm waters of Lynn Canal. The lighthouse at Point Retreat catches a ray of late afternoon sun, Eagle Glacier glistening on the mainland behind it. The beautiful Chilkat Mountains are capped in white and shrouded in summer-evening patchy clouds. The captain slows the boat, passengers and I pile onto the aft deck. Spread up and down the waterway are the dorsal fins of Killer whales. There must be more than fifty. More than sixty. In the reflected sun, their fins are dark against the water, black signals rising from the water, moving fast and disappearing, running in the water. Wolves of the sea.

The air becomes still. We become quiet. Together, we witness a sight few people ever see. We are surrounded by Killer whales. We are surrounded by freedom.

Conventional teachings of the captain and the day suggest that eternity is something that starts after death, and then goes on—well, forever. But I know that it is this moment that is eternal. One wave moves in one certain manner while that particular Killer whale rises above the water and catches one ray of light against the flash of its singular fin, its specter cradling its own lost child. I stand here on this particular boat, late in the afternoon of this certain day, with these people who have traveled distances near and far to stand here and be captured with me in this moment, which is gone before I blink and which will continue always to exist.

The captain gives the signal to be seated for our long return trip to the dock where we will offload these passengers, refuel and clean the boat, radio the dispatcher for tomorrow's schedule, and be finished with our work for this day. I will limp home, feet sore, tired, hungry, sick of bagels, wash the salt water out of my hair, lie down on the couch, talk on the phone, fall asleep. I will rise the next day to work again until the summer ends, and then I will return to the university where I am belatedly completing my education. I will see more whales and eagles, I will see rough weather and calm. I will grow older, I will grow old. I will die. And all the while, a part of me will be lost in one moment, Killer whales will surround me forever, that eternal moment will never happen again.

Ernestine Saankaláxt Hayes

Landscape with No Net Loss

This is the river's fingertip, pink bulb-end of a wild onion.
The sun leaps from the water and drops into the forest.
Bits of blown deer lichen float off without license.
I have changed a fuse in the dark. Have shoveled
trenches for cable, pulled the sway-end of a survey chain
until my palms blistered. I flirt with mosquitos in gray light,
wish I still smoked, stub my boot-toes at the marsh edge.
From the estuary, up comes the mist in faltering heat.
Longfin smelt change direction midair, belly-slap
to avoid the Chinook or shake loose eggs
or just for the hell of it, who knows, we are all
bouncing off one body and into another.
On the map, or from the treetops, the river mouth
is a hand spread wide to catch everything.

Jenifer Browne Lawrence

SALMON MOON

Surf
of moonwave,
    mist of dawn by the sea.
Mist of long lovely night ending.

The moon steps through the night.
It goes out into the south and west.
Wind comes out of the south and west.

Between sparse old shoreland spruce
    the moon is a silver wing
        in the clouds.

All night
the clouds drift over.
All night, salmon gather—
first of the run.

Robert Sund

ORCA

Rose dawn flushes our bodies, pink of a spiral shell's inner life & we are
                  surprised to be alive
                  so uncompromised & budding,

a coastline of bodies tangled like kelp in the time of water, incredible
                  to remember
                  the immensity of water:

the pigeon poop, dust & oil riding the surface streaked by cormorants
                  fanning wings of dark tides
                  & dinner,

& the plunging osprey fulfilling its specie's miracle: feathers swimming
                  grasping the silver fin of an open-mouthed
                  minnow: we all will lose in this.

Eighty-one left of your species and nine here on the shore today
                  at Fauntleroy Bay where ferries deliver
                  consciousness on a schedule of time

learned from the sun & stars, that ancient vapor stalling in carbon—
                  the smell of fuel is not blue is
                  a thick feeling—a swamp

in the bulge of stomach, or the intestines bloated with mud from the pie
                  that was rich & sweet, too
                  good to stop.

In a dream I rode a whale's back, my arms sucked to its blubber, its
                  rubber slick
                  as drenched kelp—

legless, the velocity of wind wound up in the long spring of its body,
>> a hundred yards from shore
>> my eyes squeezed against
>> ocean spray, my body the ocean

folded us under so wholly, I remembered blue for the first time
>> the address of nowhere & knowing
>> to memorize it.

No crowd here for this one-ninth of your matrilineal family, *orcinus orca*
>> of the Aleutians & San Juans
>> seeking the toothpick of Chinook salmon

in these great waters where I rub all the earth's salt on the tenderest joint
>> along your dorsal & spine
>> & you blush rose from my touch,
>> I could never do enough.

JM Miller

CARRY

For J35 Tahlequah (b. 1998)

July 4, 1999

The six of us—the boat's captain, my husband, three members of his extended family—depart LaConner in a small motorboat, riding the swift current through Deception Pass and into the Salish Sea. Excitement swirls through me like tidewater: for the first time, I am going to see orcas.

We do not, in fact, see orcas. Not in Rosario Strait, not in the open sea to the west, not at the deep trench off San Juan Island where Southern Resident pods often gather to feed on Chinook. Disappointed, we continue to Roche Harbor, cheering up at the sight of bald eagles gliding and circling above the rocky coast, so numerous we lose count.

Heading back, as we clear San Juan Island and turn east, the captain opens the throttle. The sea is smooth, and for twenty minutes we soar, carried by water, like eagles buoyed in air.

Then, the captain spots a dorsal fin. He kills the engine, and we sit silently as dozens of dorsal fins materialize and draw near from the south. Orcas surface and submerge, surface and submerge: it's J Pod, he tells us, re-oxygenating after a long feeding dive.

For the next hour, some forty orcas of every age and size slowly swirl around, even under, our boat. The captain identifies them all: giant bulls, aged matriarchs, juveniles, calf-bearing cows. Their calves.

June 26, 2009

Our adolescent niece and nephew visit from California. Our nephew's dream is to work at Sea World, training the whales he has seen perform there. We take them to Orcas Island, where we book a whale-watch tour, wanting him to view orcas living in their natural environment.

We encounter J Pod off San Juan Island's South Beach. My nephew and niece marvel at the wild orcas breeching and spyhopping just a hundred yards away. The sea is rough after the previous day's windstorm, and I spend the entire afternoon sitting cross-legged on the bow, holding our three-year-old son while he sleeps, lulled by the boat's intense rocking. In spite of the orcas' thrilling splashes and leaps, I cannot get him to wake up.

September 8, 2018

Some forty of my husband's co-workers and their families gather for a late-summer outing on a whale-watch charter sailing from Fairhaven to Friday Harbor and back. The captain warns us we may not see Southern Resident orcas; recently they've been traveling unprecedented distances, west and north, to find Chinook.

Along Sinclair Island, he identifies a family of Transient orcas traversing the shoreline: an adult male, an adult female, and her three juvenile offspring of varying sizes. Transient orcas, the captain explains, are thriving in the Salish Sea, thanks to an abundance of the marine mammals they eat.

I share binoculars with our son, now twelve. We watch the mother orca slow as her youngest calf, a yearling male, skims up her back. She swims forward, buoying him just behind her dorsal fin, while he rests.

Jennifer Bullis

INTERLUDE

She is waiting for something to end.

    Each day an extended limbo—the hiatus of a life

within a life—all spark and falter—

    ignition and idle engine. All ocean pulse

and confluence. Cliff and precipice.

How does one appropriate the life of another

    and not become a failed adagio?

Can she be courier of her weight, heartbeat to her silence,

hymn to her song—all solace and supplication?

    What wave is to moon, music is

        to lapping water.

They are the soft blur between dream

    and dream-like, this small body

and the painting of a body.

Tina Schumann

Spring Salmon at Night

I thought the west wind called me from bed
the night the river ran so hard.
I followed it over the moonlit lawn
across the road and into the woods,
climbing fallen cedars and moving
beyond the skunk cabbages. I followed
the west wind to the river bed and
plunged my legs in dark water
that sucked and swirled behind my knees
and tried to pull me beyond the bank.

And the wind stopped.
And I forgot why I came out in the night.
And I clenched the underwater moss with my toes
and was lost
until the spring salmon came,
their torpedo-shaped bodies knowing me
as another follower of currents.
In the cold gray river the spring salmon
found and circled me, their forms almost warm
as they touched the backs of my legs
guiding me back through the forest
across suburban lawns and down my own hallway
from bedroom to kitchen
until I found myself standing at the cat-food cupboard
and recognized each cat circling my legs
and my own gullibility
or desire to be lead
in the direction of someone else's hunger.

Nancy Pagh

WAYNE SUTTLES

The Orcas come, starting out slow, barely cutting the water in rhythmic time, then growing in strength as the males arrive, their dorsal fins sticking up high above the water like masts of sailboats. Soon the strait is filled with show-offs, spy hoppers and the oohs and aahs of the passengers on the boat. A super pod has arrived.

"There's Granny," the biologist calls out. We all strain to see which one is the nearly 100-year-old matriarch. "She has a gray saddle behind her dorsal fin."

The pod moves fast. I think I see Granny, but knowing that she is still alive is enough. Known for being out in front of J Pod and slapping her tail if other orcas go astray, she has fostered orphan male orcas who lost their mothers. The biologist explains that sons stay with their mothers their whole lives. Males often die within a year if they lose their mothers. Granny keeps everyone going in J Pod.

The biologist points out the latest addition to J Pod, a five-month-old calf that accompanies its mother. I don't hear his number, but he appears to be thriving. That in itself is remarkable. A great span of decades lies between Granny and the calf. There is hope for the pod's survival along with K and L Pods, if climate change and pollution don't make conditions worse for their food source, the Chinook salmon.

We stop to get a bite to eat. Then I hear, "There's Suttles." No one else on the boat responds, but I'm up on deck instantly looking for Suttles as hard as I can. I know why this orca (J40) was given this singular name: She was named for Dr. Wayne Suttles, an anthropologist who devoted his life to the study of the Coast Salish people. I lean over the rail, try to spot her with the boat's binoculars.

"Over there," the biologist says. The boat begins to move again.

It takes a while to find Suttles and focus as she moves. When she surfaces, I see a gray patch behind her dorsal fin that looks like a map of South America. She disappears, then comes back up spy hopping. I think I love her.

"How old is she?" I ask.

"She's eleven. Born in 2004. Her mother, J14, is close by. There is Hy'shqa, her older sister. J37 is on the list we gave you."

I follow J40 without the binoculars. I feel a tightness in my chest. I had heard of this orca. Know her story. To have named her after Suttles was unusual, but it shows the respect the Coast Salish have for the anthropologist. The leading authority on the ethnology and linguistics of the Coast Salish, Dr. Suttles edited the Northwest Coast volume in the Smithsonian's *Handbook of North American Indians*. Additionally, he studied and wrote about them in articles and testified as an expert witness in legal cases involving native rights in the United States and Canada. J40 was one year old when the Samish Nation named her at a potlatch in October, 2005, the same year Dr. Suttles passed away at age eighty-seven. Having worked with Dr. Suttles on an educational project years before, encountering Suttles is deeply moving for me.

The super pod moves on. Our boat follows, but there are other whale-watching boats. I soon lose sight of Suttles as the orcas tail slap and breach their way north. After two hours of encountering this wonderful family group, we head back to Friday Harbor. I wave J Pod goodbye. *Mashie, tilicum* for the joy of seeing you.

J.L. Oakley

Our One Blue Bowl

curtal sonnet

Praise this broken world, the blue within it
the water, orca, salmon, seaweed, and wrack
the crow and gull, the chip bag and butt, the boat debris.

Praise the girl for fast dip-in, the boy for skipped stone.
Praise beer cans, corks, broken buoys and rope made from hemp.
the fisherfolk and world trade for tankers, tugs and smoke.

This tidal, arched, foaming blue bowl.
This salted, sculpted, cracked blue bowl.

Savour what's moored by rope and net and hunger;
tied by hunger, heat and death. We taste

this grief, our marbled blue world.

Yvonne Blomer

THE SONG OF THE ORCA

A long time ago,
back when the oceans
were silent, and feathers of
fragments drifted wave to current,
whirl to eddy, and dribbled
slow into the cracks of the sand.
Back when darkness was the light,
and the light, therefore, was darkness.
Back even further, when the heat
of the sun was the surface of the earth,
and the earth having no surface
worth mentioning, was ashamed.

That small particle became
the world's first sound. "Which one?"
you might ask, "Which particle?" No matter.
There was a sound just the same.
And where it came from is of no concern
today, nor when it was made.

But from that sound came
the round ball, the pull of gravity, the small
bend of the horizon to the eye, the single nostril
of the whale we call the orca. This was more
than the earth could take back then,

and so this noise, the one particle of sound,
was put on hold. Kept precious and separate
from all the particles that floated
across the ocean. Other fractures splintered.
Became a sludge, a muck, an ooze
to be sucked into any fissure
provided under the darkness in the sea
known as silence. Each helix of goo
was spat out again as a thing,
an artifact, a gadget, a gathering.

When the matter of lightness
and the matter of darkness coagulated
into genes. When the genes curlicued
into the spiraling chromosomes. When the atoms
of this and aspects of that drifted together.
Whenever they stuck,
and could not pull away,
whenever the putty of life
turned traitor and added
decompostion to the process.
Whenever the egg happened,
and after. When the chromosome.
When the gene. When the atom.
When the helix.
And when the idleness and the play.
And the anger and passion.
The inspiration. When the time
came to let loose the wild orca
into the sea. That was the moment
the darkness and the light ruptured,
like a prism.

The sky lit up. The earth crusted over.
The earth was divided into half dark,
half light. Into sky and earth. Land
and sea. And the body of the orca
black and white breached and splashed.
She opened her mouth, since
she had one, and shook her
four-inch teeth. And when she calmed,
the waters around her stilled,
and she breathed in two lungs full of air.
And then she began to sing. Everywhere
the song of the orca began to be heard.
The first noise of the earth an aria now.
Unboxed. At liberty. Abundant.

An ineffable tune, lovely enough
to be unending, and final. The song
of the orcas. The light and the dark
together.

This is the song
that has begun to disappear,
hushed, has moved toward silence
again. The song that might be saved.

Anita K. Boyle

ECHOLOCATION

Honolulu, Hawai'i

My wife nurses our newborn,
while I feed our toddler.
On the news, we watch you balance

your dead calf on your rostrum.
They numbered you because
there are so few left in your pod.

They named you native
because your kind is vanishing.
My family, too, comes from the sea,

and the fish our ancestors
depended on are also endangered.
Days pass. We drive our eldest

to preschool, the youngest
to her vaccinations. You carry
your decomposing daughter

a thousand nautical miles until
every wave becomes an elegy,
until our planet becomes an open

casket. What is mourning
but our shared echolocation?
Today, you let go. Today, you let

fall. We wish we could honi you,
breathe in your breath, offer
small comfort. How do you say,

"sorry," in your dialect of sonar,
calls, and whistles? Nights pass.
You keep swimming across

the Salish Sea. We carry our girls
into the Pacific. They kick and laugh
when embraced by salt water. We

wish they could see you breach
and dive so they can grow
in the wake of your resilience.

We promise to tell them your story
so they'll remember that love
is a wild, oceanic instinct.

Craig Santos Perez

BALLARD LOCKS

Air-struck, wound-gilled, ladder
  upon ladder of them thrashing
through froth, herds of us climb
  the cement stair to watch
this annual plunge back to dying, spawn;
  so much twisted light
the whole tank seethes in a welter of bubbles:
  more like sequined
purses than fish, champagned explosions
  beneath which the ever-moving
smolt fume smacks against glass, churns them up
  to lake from sea level, the way,
outside, fishing boats are dropped or raised
  in pressured chambers, hoses spraying
the salt-slicked undersides a cleaner clean.
  Now the vessels
can return to dock. Now the fish,
  in their similar chambers, rise and fall
along the weirs, smelling the place
  instinct makes for them,
city's pollutants sieved
  through grates: keeping fish
where fish will spawn, but changing the physics of it,
  changing ours as well:
one giant world encased
  with plastic rock, seaweed transplanted
in thick ribbons for schools to rest in
  before they work their way up
the industrious journey: past
  shipyard, skyline, playground;
past bear-cave, past ice-valley; past the place
  my father's father would,
as a child, have stood with crowds
  and shot at them with guns

then scooped them from the river with a net, such
   silvers, pinks cross-hatched in black:
now there's protective glass
   behind which gray shapes shift: change
then change again. Can you see the jaws
   thickening with teeth, scales
beginning to plush themselves with blood; can you see
   there is so little distinction here
between beauty, violence, utility?
   The water looks like boiling sun.
A child has turned his finger into a gun.
   Bang, the ladders say
as they bring up fish into too-bright air, then down again,
   while the child watches the glass
revolve its shapes into a hiss of light.
   Bang, the boy repeats.
His finger points and points.

Paisley Rekdal

Pantoum for Tahlequah

August 2018

I can't sleep and when I dream, I dream of her
carrying her daughter, 17 months she bore,
swimming the dark waters of the Salish Sea,
dark sea that carries us all equally.

She will carry her daughter 17 days,
bearing her grief, searching for salmon
in the dark sea that carries us all equally,
in these waters, her birthright.

She bears her grief as they search for salmon,
swims past the bays where their mothers were taken,
in these waters, their birthright,
waters that glisten, hide sewage and toxins.

Swims past the bays where their mothers were taken,
up the coast they've long swum,
in these waters that glisten, hide sewage and toxins,
carrying grief she can't set down.

Fewer each year, up the coast they swim.
Does she feel grief for her species as they face?
Carrying grief she won't set down,
in this sea where they've hunted, quiet, alone.

Yes, it is grief for her species facing extinction
in a warming sea that first was their home,
this sea where they've hunted quiet, alone.
She carries our grief, what we can't set down

in this warming sea that first was their home;
how long will she carry her grief—
our grief, what we can't set down—
that we are changing our world *and* theirs.

How long will we carry the grief,
her grief and ours, knowing that
we've changed our world and theirs?
How long can we carry this on?

Holly J. Hughes

ORCAS IN PASSING

I forced my kayak through chop and riptide to chase my childhood dream of seeing wild orcas. Our group of tourists and naturalists were traveling along San Juan Island's west coast where salmon swam through ocean forests of kelp that snatched my paddle and entangled my rudder. I was thirty-five but felt as if I were a child greedy for a glimpse, and another, and another. The whales stayed at the edge of sight.

We reached calm water. Our guide signaled a stop. I flexed stiff fingers. I massaged red palms. I dipped swollen hands into seawater and shook cold drops into a breeze that blew across my face. When I was a child, I had imagined jumping off jetties and gliding into deep sea dives only to be discovered by orcas who would recognize a kindred spirit, swim beside me, lift me onto their backs so that I could grasp a six-foot dorsal fin and ride among them as brave and strong and remarkable as they, and not the all-too-ordinary girl my parents, sister, teachers, and classmates laughed and swore I was. The usual childhood fantasies, I suppose, but stories of the orcas' intelligence and gentle nature remained an inspiration as I grew into adulthood, became a naturalist, and now leaned back and scanned the horizon. I had good reasons for optimism. Over a decade of Puget Sound orca captures had finally ended in the mid-1970s. The Southern Residents had lost nearly a third of their number, but this was the early 1990s, and the orcas were in a population boom, albeit a brief one.

My kayak swayed gently. Black-mottled harbor seals popped silvery heads above water and eyed us from a distance. Behind our kayaks came a sound as if a dozen people exhaled at once. I twisted around in my cockpit so fast I almost capsized. A flat sea shaded from sparkling turquoise to forest green. We exchanged looks. We'd all heard it. But now there was silence.

I turned toward the bow and scanned where we'd last seen whales. Again came that rush of air from behind. I looked sternward. Again came silence and water at rest. Then I heard my heart pound. Three orcas arose so swiftly the sea scarcely rippled. The whales plunged downward, disappeared, rose again, and arced down dead behind me straight on course to smash my kayak when they next surfaced.

I stared at dark water. I hoped those childhood stories were true and orcas didn't attack people or boats. Two whales surfaced beside my kayak. One was close enough to touch. It wasn't just fear that held back my hand. The orcas took no more notice of me than I would of driftwood. They were in their element; I was far from mine and no longer a child. We could meet on the border between our worlds but only for a moment before going our separate ways.

The whales swam off. We paddled hard after them. We never caught up.

Adrienne Ross Scanlan

STEAL YOURSELF

A family full of predators,
the silent, sinister kind,
everyday on land, a strange mix
charming interplay between snipes.

A pod of ballenas asesinas,
distinctly black-backed, white patch above eyes,
moves with intention atop the food chain,
never known to harm humans.

Predators with legs, without conscience,
grope in deep waters, large hands
capable of stealing youth, in the middle
of their morning swim.

In sea green chambers, a mother's eyes stay open,
powerless witness, she wails her melodic pleas.
Keeping busy—in the mother tongue—
she calls her babies home.

I still recall the lurid nightmares, years
after fleeing my native Florida, always stuck
at the door of my teens, captive like *Tokitae*,
truth hiding in shadows, my mother, nowhere.

And Orcas, born from protective wombs,
glide with grace, massive apex predators,
fulfilling Nature's call. But human hands, swift with nets,
claim calves, at once stolen, then dispersed.

How a dorsal fin is pliable, like childhood.

JS Nahani

TIDES OF MATERNITY

a tanka sequence

I overdosed
on the mothering hormone
after giving birth
oxytocin carried me out
on waves of oceanic bliss

at a workshop
for nursing mothers
returning to work
the fear of separation
profound depths of sorrow

dropping her son off
for his freshman year
in celebration
my old friend and I
go whale-watching

not ready
he drops out of college
the orca pod
we watched that day
no longer thrives

fathomless grief
the killer whale carried
her dead child
for a thousand miles
calling us to bear witness

Sheila Sondik

RETURN TO SALISH SEA

At sunset, the sky was salmon on fire.
I sat in pebbled sand
and watched cedars rise and fall
in sections of time.

My basalt backbone curved
and skin split.
Lungs became gills.
Saltwater left imprints on cells
marking this ocean as home.

Christine Clarke

FLOW

as if the wind
brought her closer
whale spray

crescent moon
sinking into the bay
fin of an orca

mouth of the river
dawn and a damselfly alight
on a blade of grass

a leaf
caught in an eddy
salmon run

culvert
the creek choked
with salmon

Seren Fargo

INSTRUCTIONS ON BEING A SEA CREATURE

If you are a whale, your mouth
should be in your forehead,
not to mention your blowhole
gasping exclamations nearby!
If not, then you may need gills
folded like taffy and oxygenated.
Besotted, Pliny the Elder
declared a dolphin's tongue
better than those of most humans
of his acquaintance. You should be
so lucky. Your eyes may migrate,
fleeing the symmetry of your face
or you may never sleep again.
Say good bye to opposable thumbs.
On the other hand (so to speak),
you get to spawn thousands.
Practice lurking, breaching,
crushing ship hulls like cellophane.
Who else finds their way by singing?

Allen Braden

What We Heard About the Sea

Once we belonged. We belonged for wet
millenniums. We exiled ourselves

gill by gill. The sea sang us forth,
first birth, first Eden,

our blood tide brackish. The Fall
was a struggle to shore, sip of sharp air.

We can't even name how we long to go home,
but still that desire

swims in us. We return to visit
with buoyancy compensators, masks

and tanks of air, we sink, remember
how it felt to live here,

but we are tourists now. Cold gold
light in water, we touch brittle fingers

of black coral, feathered tongues of barnacles,
even the great wings of manta rays

soar over us. We suck hungrily
on our mouthpieces, swallowing back our salt,

yearning for the time when we lived here,
when we could fly.

Rachel Rose

DEAR BABY BO

Let me tell you about the first time I saw a killer whale. One year, we drove the long hours from Chicago to Orlando so my mother, your ya-ya, could meet up with old classmates from Thailand. To entertain the rambunctious boy I was, my father took me to Sea World, a place I cannot bring myself to go to anymore. A place I now see as an abuse to the natural existence of things. But I cannot lie. That first time, when I was six or seven, was magic. To say something is magic or magical seems banal nowadays. But every time we delve into memory, any memory, it is a bit like magic, the reaching into a hat to pull forth the rabbit of a moment. My father and I sat in the large outdoor amphitheater, surrounded by excited families. I was excited. Why wouldn't I be? I had touched a stingray. Had watched dolphins jump through hoops and observed colorful fish swim in neon tanks. Had eaten a lot of candy and soda so my body was in sugar overdrive. Waiting for the show to start, however, I grew tired. The Florida heat wore me down. I was thankful to be sitting and leaning against my father in the same way you do when fatigue comes to you. Then the show started. Loud music. Loud voice over loud speakers. And at first, nothing. The sunlight danced on the surface of the water. There was a hush of anticipation, the silent build up of something special. And then magic. A black fin cleaved the water. The black bump of a nose. The expulsion of water from a blowhole. "This," said the loud voice over loud speakers, "is Shamu, the killer whale." Instead of joining the excited chorus of awe, I cried. I was so close to Shamu. In the front row, on wet bleacher seats. I was witness to this otherworldly creature, sleek and shimmering, skin reflecting the late day sun. Shamu leapt into the air, twirling and twisting, water gliding off its body. Magic. I had not realized I held my breath. But I did. I held my breath and cried. Impossible. But impossible was possible because a killer whale danced in and out of water, because it moved in rhythm to its trainer in a tight bodysuit. My father sat beside me, hands on his knees, laughing that hyena laugh that drew the attention of the other kids. He was so caught up in the moment, so moved by Shamu, he did not see his boy crying. When Shamu flopped onto the water, water splashed four rows up. It was like a baptism, even though I had not a clue what a baptism was. I only knew we were soaked with water a killer whale had propelled out of its pool. And the water was cold. And the cold felt like magic. Finally, my father looked down and noticed my tears. "It's OK," he said. "It can't hurt you." I cried so hard I could not tell him I was not afraid of the killer whale. "Don't believe the name," he said. "Killer whale will not kill you." I cried so hard I could not tell him I was not afraid of being killed by a killer whale. I could not tell him because my throat tightened the way it does when a cry comes over you. A couple of the kids around me asked if I was OK, but my father told them I was fine, just scared. When the show was over, some of the workers at Sea World handed us towels to dry off. "My son," my father said to them, "thought the killer whale was going to jump out of the water and eat him." I did not tell them the truth, either, which was this: what made me weep was the animal itself. How beautiful it was, how enormous, swimming in a pool and not an ocean. It was beauty contained. It was beauty that choked the breath. Beauty that made me cry. I think I knew beauty like this was fleeting. Beauty like this would someday be gone. And then it would become a story. There are so many stories of things lost. Stories are where they live again. I tell you this story because I dreamed a killer whale tonight. Because there are not many killer whales left. Because when you get older there may be no more killer whales. But that dream—it felt like that first time. Magic. Just watching Shamu swim and be. I woke up crying. May you find, son, something that holds your breath and makes you weep. May you one day be so moved.

Your Father

Ira Sukrungruang

MOTHEROGRAPHY

Before—

      the bone minerals of old barnacles clung,

             the winter skies grew vagrant,

        a child named its stillness. Before

what passes when all else has passed.

           A coastline, lain flat, fell behind.

The smell of rain taught the world where it would fall.

      The hollow rhythm of something mourned

         was the hour that emptied a child from the well

inside a mother. The gasp of a god

           as the body let go. Force, like an ocean,

that grows. Before a woman dragged herself from a wound

      to arrive on someone else's tongue.

The wind tells a story

           that touches thousands of mouths

long before a mother is something forsaken

      by wind. A story of weight.

            Of distance. Of feral songs.

Chelsea Dingman

INDIVISIBLE

In the river's cold passage
      a flash of undulant silver
          beyond my drift,
flickering skin
      of a spring Chinook
         snagged
on a sunken branch
      and loyally motioning,
         wavy surges
that let slip the deal driven,
      the endings we live
         in every shudder
of the dam-run current.

Derek Sheffield

IN THIS BLOOD, A LUSH COTILLION

I tell my children one droplet of fog bears
thousands of nutrients. What rain rinses from rock
slips through aqueous bloodstream. A stone is a
surface aching for lichen. We all want to live,
feet muddied from wading, the wonder of mayflies
fresh on our lips.

In our veins, a lush cotillion
of southern chemicals, local history coagulates
into heritage. The truth of Alabama includes
polychlorinated biphenyls, unspeakable
endocrine symptoms, the body of Terry Baker
buried at 16 from brain and lung cancer bloomed
by PCBs. This history is poison we can't erase
this legacy of long-time Monsanto, quiescent
inside organs. A matter of time
is a broken heart is a leaf floating downstream;
an undercurrent of invisible toxins linking
us to southern resident orcas.

I imagine my fellow mammalian mother
balancing on her head the dead baby
for seventeen days. Imagine grief so deep
we are all of us carriers,
secret harbors for chemicals restricting development of reproductive
systems, gutting immune function, ending the possibility
of new life. Imagine the word *pro-life*
covering corporate poison we can't erase with
sweet tea and solvents. I have nothing
to tell the children, or their spy-hopping
sisters. I save these words for
those who birthed them.

I save the story for a brass plaque
beneath a monument honoring blood:
lush cotillion of stone-faced toxins,
stiff tower of dying mammal babies,
what kills our orca relatives
naturally must kill us.

Alina Stefanescu

DEAR ZYGOTE

Let us let X = *mammalian I*,
and to boot an old friend,

which is what chinks us to Melville's
　　　　Queequeg, whom Ishmael
half-morphs his way into simply

by thinking around about glyphs
　　　　harpooned on Q's skin. That
Möbius strip of a person! That prince-

covered code—the ship's crux.
　　　　His wooden doll treatise makes
kindness suggest *Let's go make rainbow*

fish from these minnows!
　　　　Maybe we always only just
needed more liminal structures

from which to untangle mind's lures:
　　　　To re-feel the ways Queequeg
calls us to cradle new berths for pain

in ways that might lurch us more
　　　　toward the good. In short, Q
calls us to be full-on mammal assisters

in this surliest era—whose purlieu
　　　　can clearly be said
to suffer the Ahab Complex.

Queequeg's epiderm-text basically
　　　　pray-asks whoever picks up a pen
to rewrite the word. Repeat motifs

of joyride beauty. Who wouldn't
       prefer to queue up
one's crypto-adventure across the

blaze of each limb, if only to showcase
       such blue raw gnosis-explosion?
It's a little bit *krill swarm*. It's a little like mother *Tahlequah*.

Diane Raptosh

THE END OF THE ROAD FROM NANTUCKET

This is the end of the whaleroad...

—Robert Lowell

I.

Dark. Dark, and winds
lash the rains into frenzy.
The whole continent sleeps
its bloody sleep of history
with dreams of Sitting Bull
and Joaquin Murrietta,
keelboats and outcasts
from this coast of no story
all the way back to the glory
of Nantucket. The orcas
cry into the Sound, rise
through dark-swirled water,
and plunge again, and still
the unappeasable fears,
the hard rain and wind
of desperate sea-locked men
ride out the winter storm.

II.

Dogfish slowly, slowly spin
beneath the waves. Friends, the
ancient gillnetter weeps
into the nets he mends. No mystery
to his craft: a lull
can promise fortune or get a
fisherman killed. What outlasts
the sea is praise. Glory
slides into a sailor's eyes all hoary,
weather-worn and wry, a causeway
of human years. No Blighs,
no Ahabs survive to trouble water

on this coast. We will
ourselves no future, we steer
a course unmarked by dorsal fin
or blow-hole that gives again
and again each day a style, a form.

III.
Dark. Dark, and dark winds
swirl from the past. Wednesday
when we die, the sea will weep
no more, the lethal blistering
tides will rise into a fullbodied
swell lifting the last regatta
into doomsday, the masts
shattered like the Pequod's forty
fathoms into hell. For we
who have no past or cause,
the seas fill our eyes
with the hunger for slaughter,
a taste for the manly thrill
of whale blood, the sea's veneer,
of dying whales that win
no wars, no time, no gain.
It's a human name we give the storm.

Sam Hamill

ARTICULATIONS

Once this whale moved through wild waves.
Now its bones are artifacts, fleshing
out our dreams of planetary dominion.
Imagine this being, resonating to the curve

of voices, calling out its watery expectations,
adapting to the liquid choreography
of the moon's insistence. Through all this
it remained true to its synaptic alliances, abandoning

the land, subscribing to the pulse of oceanic time,
penetrating dark voids that we have forgotten,
clinging precariously to a magmatic existence
that is never quiet, that expands, falls away,

changes form, this elusive being, this eternal
wanderer, still articulating the dark interior
of our imagination, this creature now fallen prey
to chaotic change, its long voyage abruptly ended

on this white wall of silence.

Jim Milstead

MAY WE NOT FORGET THE WHALE

There floated into my inmost soul, endless processions of the whale.
—Herman Melville

...great heavens of whales in the waters...
—David Herbert Lawrence

White horses gamboling over
Haro Strait, a wave train
Amidst islands, curling white
Looped between shores
Everlasting, evermore.

Mary Elizabeth Gillilan

Self-Portrait as Southern Resident Orca

For everybody *I'm speechless Damn it I gotta go get my camera!*
For *this must be the happiest pod.*
For you can hear them saying *there she goes again. Big one! Wow!*
For you can hear them clapping, laughing.

For I am made of the research proving there is no difference
in the lifespan
of an orca born at SeaWorld
and an orca born in the wild.

For behind me 700,000 years of genetic distinction.
For behind me 700,000 years of a distinct dialect evolving.

For I was misnamed whale killer by Spanish explorers.
For I am a dolphin.

For each year I ingest some of the seven million quarts of motor oil
that washes into the Salish Sea.

For PCBs were banned in 1979, but each day I push
through
1.5 billion pounds of them.

For in my fat stores I carry your legacy of coal mining,
electrical appliance dependence, your attempts at insect eradication.

For because of you I brush up against carcinogenic furans.

For I am a mother carrying her dead newborn.

For I have been carrying her for days.

For thanks to my contaminated milk, she is even more toxic than I.

FOR LOVE OF ORCAS

For you might call this behavior a tour of grief, but I've been driving her
to the surface so she can take a breath.

For my solitude grows scarce.

For the noise of passing ships interferes
with my clicks, my whistles, my pulses.
With finding salmon—species, speed, size.

For the sea and I are both wide.

For the water I glide through is poisoned with viscosity index improvers;
for the lapping is laced with alkaline additives and sealants;
for if you read more closely, you will learn PCBs were not banned
but permitted in lower concentrations.

For I can certainly experience intense emotion.

For Monsanto's CEO makes 19 million a year
but the Chemical Action Plan lacks funding.

For there is no government strong enough to save me.

For behold my spyhopping!

For who can resist my one-syllabled, Darth Vader-like exhale?

For Google *biomagnification*.

For the rainbowed road is my demise.

For the highway's yellow line, I die.

For I am corralled not by my mistakes but yours.

For the doors of my duration are closing.

Martha Silano

#LOVELETTERFORYOUANDTAHLEQUAH

Small dog froze on slatted stairs. You carried him, hooves kicking chest. This was the test that started us. I had to learn you on the lam. In the slit, key cards glowed green. Light opened every door, meaning the only door, meaning move forward. The secret film unfurled its secret score.

•

Sometimes a room becomes red hills. You unzip on the overlook, thumbing belt loops. Away from Twitter, I forget we might die. Why are we still wearing towels? At breakfast, you seem upset I'm eating like a bird. But birds eat worms. Granola's just this thing with nerves. I'll eat anything you say it is.

•

Stopped mid-climb up No Name Hill, you snap photos, ladders to nowhere. We're both men in the tenderness department. That story about nets catches my breath. Marine mammals strangle, tangled in smaller catch. We watch through Plexiglas as salmon leap fish ladders.

•

Today you're someone else and I'm pure pelt. "Pirates do it," skull on a flag. Now we're floating on a ship, adrift. Anything might be a shark, or suffocate in plastic bags, swirling whirlpools of trash.

•

landscape with bodies
silicon parts
our gender
reveal
cake
reveals

      yes (fireworks)
      yes (swoon)
      yes (bending forth)

•

Gyrating blades, propeller rimmed in yellow tape: one misstep might cost a limb, or fly to Sequim, Winthrop, Naches. I carry on down tarmac. You're the city at the end of the gate. For you I board the tiny plane without in-flight magazines or coffee in Styrofoam cups. For you I sit in a bumpy seat and dig my nails into blue upholstery. For you I rise into the smoky haze, forests burning north, east, and south. For you I look west, past Tahlequah carrying her calf. For you I switch seats with one who wants so badly to sit with another. For you I am home from work and hungry. For you I am working with tools. For you I feed chickens. For you I wait and wear a dress and listen for your car in the garage. For you I am serving dinner on a blue-and-orange plate. For you I imagine a body you will never have. For you I imagine my body and it is not the body I have. For you I cut plastic six-pack rings to pieces. For you I twist inside the gyre.

Carol Guess

TO THESE LEGACY CHEMICALS

The global manufacture of PCBs corresponded well
with symbols and error bars
near the highly industrialized areas.

The world's killer whale populations
ranged widely—
males and females, respectively.

Alaskan offshore, Faroe Islands, and Iceland.
Hawaii, Japan, Northeast Pacific,
Strait of Gibraltar, and U.K.

Indeed, a long list
for other persistent contaminants to generate
as fish stocks and seal populations fluctuate over time.

We compiled available data.
Risk categories were set based on predicted growth rates
evaluated against forecast.

Each plot represents
a long-lived marine apex predator
not included here.

The coming 100 years:
light and dark green circles;
accumulation and loss.

Bold lines and shading
(mother-calf transfer)
regardless of location.

Despite sharing the same coastline
the status-quo efforts
are yet to be destroyed.

Sarah DeWeerdt

Spiritus: Inside Speiden Channel

First we saw only the humps of their backs, two black curves just above the water. Was it...? A breathing ocean creates many illusions, and so at first we tempered our hope. Dappled diamonds of light flashed on the water as our kayaks bobbed along the shimmering waves. We scanned the sea. Nothing but the blue blue of water and sky. Just a mirage, we thought, those black curves on the horizon. We were in the open channel between Roche Harbor and Stuart Island in Washington's San Juans, our paddles and kayaks straining against a wind we'd been unprepared for. I tried to focus on the Olympic Mountains, on Vancouver Island. But we seemed not to be gaining on the landscape we aimed for, and I could feel frustration building.

Mirage. But no, there they were again, this time clearly visible, moving easily through the water, moving toward us. Miraculous, it seemed, that we alone were seeing them; normally, during the height of summer, whale-viewing boats would see them first, and gather. But we were just a small group, sitting low on the water. Our own private viewing. We pulled our kayaks together, holding each other's paddles to remain close. Two of the orcas, a female and her offspring, came to within a hundred yards. We could hear them, the whoosh of their exhalations, could see the white ovals behind their eyes. Suddenly, synchronized, they jumped, their graceful bodies momentarily above the water before they dove, disappearing beneath the surface.

Gone too was the earlier frustration.

I thought immediately of that day when I read about Tahlequah, of the grief that propelled her to carry her dead calf for seventeen days and roughly a thousand miles through the water. I did not learn until later the extent of the loss, that her grief was not hers alone. That Tahlequah's pod was endangered, and the baby she carried represented the latest in a series of unsuccessful births; that approximately 75% of newborns in the Southern Resident orca population in the previous two decades had not survived; that there have been no viable offspring in over three years. The reasons are largely human caused: dams that hinder the spawning of Chinook salmon; toxic polychlorinated biphenyls (PCBs) which, though banned over thirty years ago, linger in orcas' food sources; noise from ships and other vessels that interfere with orca echolocation necessary for predation and communication. This is not an issue confined to Tahlequah's pod. It is estimated that orca populations worldwide will decrease by up to fifty percent in the next 30-50 years.

That day, we had scanned the water, hoping to see the orcas again, but they were gone. It didn't matter. Inspired, our spirits had changed. Spirit. From the Latin *spiritus*: to breathe. Related to *inspirer*: to breathe life into. To be filled with grace.

Who do we become once such grace is forever depleted?

How easily, despite the still steady winds, we'd paddled through the rest of that afternoon, beneath cirrostratus clouds and water-color blue skies.

Daryl Farmer

CENTRAL HEALING

After many Moons, people divested of all but their dignity arrive
knees and backs bend to stick hands into oily waters:

> *On sacred tribal lands*
> *Bear Dancers circle round*
> *Bend, grunting toward the ground*

world leaders sweat beneath the Sun to save sea life and gulls
oil execs and railroad owners strain their muscles to vacuum up debris

wall streeters trade themselves to protect the riches of the sea
even journalists stop their broadcasts to plant, harvest and seed

> *White sage smolders*
> *Drums beat and Elders speak*
> *Of wintering the past*

for beyond Katrina, beyond tsunamis
beyond depletion of herring, sea scooters, salmon and orcas

beyond deregulations, housing foreclosures, lost savings
beyond meager health care, minor energy reforms

> *Give your pain to the Bears*
> *Give it up to the fire*
> *Flames crackle, spark and rise*

beyond contamination of world-wide food supplies
beyond viral buyouts of commerce, media, banks

beyond nuclear meltdowns, trains de-railing
carbon counts rising, glaciers melting, oceans warming

> *Give your pain to the Bears*
> *Give it up to the fire*
> *Drums beat and Elders speak*

beyond the blow out of safety valves on the pipes of democracy
beyond the sludge of remorse, the rattle of bones

Mother Time draws the line at Cherry Point and Salish Sea
home of tribal wisdoms and sovereign treaties

> *Give your pain to the Bears*
> *Give it up to the fire*
> *We mourn, shuffle, weave and dance*

and in this far west corner, we the people of many nations
beholden, as we are, to the great Salish Sea

recall the taste of wild salmon, waters safe for drinking
clean air, and old growth trees

> *Give your pain to the Bears*
> *Give it up to the fire*
> *We trail, track, circle round*

and as Sun and Moon rise over Time's rail line,
hearts pulse and echo nature's drum beats …

> *We trail, track, circle round*
> *Bend grunting toward the ground*
> *Flames of love spark and rise*

and with a Motherly rush, we return like salmon, swim upstream
restoring Mother Earth's forests, rivers and seas

> *Love abounds in Elder nations*
> *Love abounds in citizen nations*
> *On planet earth, love abounds.*

Betty Scott

FOR THE CREATURES OF THE SEA

Memory is this: a small fish
in a man's pocket. The tide turning in

on itself. The sea is too large
to be contained. One can never get

enough. Jung says the dead
assign all their work to the living.

Do we ever see clearly enough? Water
has no regret. Has no will to give us pain.

A fish's eye. A fish's gill.
A small thing next to the heart.

Terry Ann Carter

BECOMING ANADROMOUS

Who needs fire? We are two kinds of water, you in aqua
marine tuxedo, and I in a freshwater dress, skimming floor
once more before they pull the plug, send us swirling down

dawn, trail of oil rainbowing beneath your bike.
I'll learn to lean into you, how to ride out an earthquake
in your bed, the scent of melons sending us sleepwise. Seismic

is what we call ourselves, tsunamis, cliff jumpers missing
for weeks. It's no surprise we've become shoeless, naked
with all that walking, all this steam. Vapor is vapor,

but the language of lines raked in earth speaks
of Yellow Finns and beets, of fence lines, foundations: all things
rooted. Give me your feet. I'll fill a bowl with river, with dirt,

my thumbs divining your Achilles Heel. If the tide charts are true
we'll find a way to come together, when the land bridge returns, once
every never. I'll fill five canvases with Atlantic and Cutthroat,

you'll write your field guide to bladder wrack and kelp. Contrary
to popular belief, we're connected, Chinook living on
in the sea for years before returning.

Ronda Piszk Broatch

OCEAN FUGUE

the orca pod
forced to maneuver
a labyrinth of nets
scarcely able to take
one quick breath

small boats
racing to circle misty
exhalations—
a matriarch spy hops,
seeking a way out

each year
fewer orcas come to play
off the bay—
the newest of the pod
may remain nameless

through the fog
a four voice fugue
of wet breaths—
the rise and descent
of passing whales

Carole MacRury

SINKING

there are those of us
at the bow of the boat
breathing deeply
eyes front
teeth bared
for anything

and those
at the stern watching
what was
disappear with the wake

and the dwindling orcas
who would say
if they could

      there are too many boats
      heedless

      no matter the gaze

Luther Allen

PULL OF THE MOON

I paddled where currents converged
from the sides of a narrow island.

The tide, coursing hard, rejoined
itself in a churn south of the spit

formed, I guessed, by centuries
of just such motion. Hordes of froth

collided. Schools of bright herring boiled
the surface—a mob of gulls bobbed,

hovered, dove, and stuffed their gullets
on those silvery swarms. The sizzle

drew in a few gleaming salmonid nomads
breaching ecstatic.... I was lost

in the thrall. There'd be no paddling
back to the beach till the slack,

so I drifted and turned like a twig
of cliff-side madrona blown from a shore,

tossed and soaked but safe enough
in the troughs of the chop. I remember

this when I think of us, what we call
our attraction—pull of the moon

on the one sea, its reunion, once
the land's no longer between us.

Jed Myers

DIVE

What songs carried you
as you carried your calf,
dead half a month,
through sunstruck waves?

You must have bruised
as you balanced her
on your forehead—grief's
dense-boned body is built
like yours, for diving.

What words do you hold
for *first breath*, for *almost*,
for water warming too fast,
Chinook sliding higher
into deltas to disappear,

for the deafening drone
of freighters and fishing dories,
ferries where whale watchers
clamber at the rail
to see, before you're lost,
how something can be built
of so much breath?

Orca, God
of the Underworld
we named you
in a dead language,
watching you breach
and plunge, your skin
wet smoke below
slate-gray waves—

but you're only bone
and blood, grief
and salt water, like us.
Each time, exhausted,
you let her slip

you dived again—
hauled what you had lost
back to the light. Tahlequah,
teach us to see what shouldn't
be buried, to speak its name
across dark waters
and hear, as you can hear,
what echoes back.

Ryler Dustin

WHALE WATCHING

The morning's fog is thick as frosted glass.
Every wave's shadow and sea-drifting log
breathes innuendo. Strain eyes to their limits, ears
perched alert for the spurt of water to signal

their surfacing. A pod of females follows her
through the Salish Sea, hunting for Chinook salmon.
Walk the half-mile trail south to north, north
to south, south to north. Commandeer a picnic bench

and wait, unpack sandwiches, stare at water,
and don't dare let your eyes wander.
Hike up to the lighthouse and wait.
Hike down to the old kiln and wait.

Seals. Moss. Purple starfish big as backpacks.
Pull out binoculars. Cameras. And wait.
Watch for her girls club, imagine her sleek
dorsal fin higher than our heads, her black back

like a moving hill, weaving in and out of water,
sewing big stitches in the dark blue bay.
She's circling round these islands
where we live our little lives.

Her massive grace. Her godsome body.

Dayna Patterson

FULL MOON BEACH WALK, INCOMING

Clamped all day against sunlight, barnacles
open to the salt tide at dusk. The Sound
sloshes an imprint on Foulweather Bluff,
a pair of buffleheads upend in unison.
Snails the shade of mulberries loosen underwater.
Unlacing their boots, two beach hikers
wade barefoot around the jutting bank,
waves sluicing their legs. A conglomeration of kelp,
eelgrass, plastic bottles, shotgun shells, clams,
and footprints muddy the king tide opus.
A toddler in a lime tutu holds tight to her father's thumb.
Harbor porpoise cut a scalloped ribbon offshore.
Joy is the fly on this peach pit, is a violet-backed swallow
chasing the heron. Fragrant as a wet dog,
it shakes and pants, drops a piece of driftwood at your feet,
then races into the waves, trusting
that you will pick up and throw the stick.

Jenifer Browne Lawrence

LIME KILN

We watched the pod pass at Lime Kiln point,
standing together, a family of five, as an otter
emerged and remained fixed on the waterline;

his eyes not towards the milling people in the park,
but eying those larger black and white bodies
making their ponderous way north, mostly invisible,

but the machines tracking their movements told
the Ranger who told us to stay, so we stayed.
They came, with a few boats behind, everything else

out of the way, like the otter flapping his paws
quietly in the water, watching. The black fins
rising straight up, sinking, like a machine needle,

or exclamation points, and I thought of Merwin's
extinction poem, *one must always pretend something
among the dying,* and have always thought thus

one must always pretend, though under summer skies
today, and high clouds there is nothing staged
in the otter's caution, in the breaths from the sea—

relief, shock, awe, or all three, percussive as they came.
Then gone, they were gone. And the otter. Though
we know where they are, like stars turning back to stone.

And of the mother carrying her still born the captain
said, "it's almost human," but after seventeen days
every parent knows, that's the most animal in us all.

Jeremy Voigt

STRANGER

In a 100 years wild salmon runs south of Canada will be reduced to remnant runs.
—Bob Lackey, Professor of Fisheries at Oregon State University

Future children will hear the story of when
a stranger wandered into town armed with harp,
got food, lodging, women, disappeared
and became a legend.

"Years passed, and someone found a blood-stained
knife under moss beside harp, strings gone
but ghost music still playing in alders and firs."

The truth will become
the stranger, which was salmon,
changed into man, river a harp,
when real story of losing salmon and orcas
grew too sad to tell.

Scott T. Starbuck

MELTDOWN

It was all somehow accounted for
in the ledgers of those who served

the kings and commissars of an orderly
distribution and control

that everything was theirs, even the crushed
knuckles of the stones, even the stiff

facsimiles of our brethren who had vanished
before us into that green flash

above the sundown sea. The whales, the dodo,
the great apes, all irrelevant as beauty, disappeared

like beauty, leaving only their names scratched
next to our own in the halls of unopening books.

We might have prayed for God
to come, or Noah, and deliver us

two by two again, drowning our terrible machines.
Now the oceans rise to take us

all. The stars go out. The angels, weary of extinctions.
Shake their heads. But what were we to do, force

the powerful to change?

Christopher Howell

A Sailor Writes to Me About the Sea

He smells a hint of leather
mixed with salt and oil, pictures home

like it never was or ever will be again.
He forgets that every time

waves arrive and leave,
they revisit pebbles—

their labor and promise,
smoothed for interpretation.

Nima Kian

FOR SCARLET

Pulled from your mother
by the teeth of your kin,
maybe a grandmother or aunt,
you were midwifed by love
and fierce need
into the cold diaspora
of economic progress.

From once teeming blue Eden
we made for you a ghost sea,
a liquid barrens haunted by hunger,
engine prowl, dead zones.
A few generations of forgetting
was all it took.

You learned the songs anyway
and leapt like any beloved child.
Seven months old, you performed sixty breaches
when your family returned to the Salish Sea.

Tourists cheered from whale-watching boats
while from more practical vessels
biologists noted your small size
and sub-average growth. Three summers later
you were emaciated, falling behind.

By summer's end all three tribes of your kind
gathered near Race Rocks, and you were not there.
The unplanted garden of you
lay somewhere below.

Was our God watching
when you could go no farther
and began to sink?

Were there angels
in the darkening columns of water?
Or was it just cold, human betrayal
all the way down?

Rest in peace, brief pearl,
little prophet.

May we do everything but.

Rob Lewis

WEAPON

It's going to take forever—the rest of our lives, one after another global catastrophe & I'm embarrassed to say in some ways it will be a relief: just end it already, & let the future critters take their wet breaths. The seabird autopsies kill me. I mean they kill everyone—I had vowed to stop saying that things kill me after D asked me if I would kill so-and-so if they did such-and-such minor thing. I can't even remember & it's about killing for godssake. Lately she says to me:

weaponnnnn

in a whispery, sinister voice
& it chills me, Jesus Christ it chills me. I ask her, what is a weapon & she replies it is something that flies through the air, my friends play it at school:

weaponnnnn

I'm not one I create what
nature does better—evolve or metastasize to block the sun, that thing, that thing—that toothless teratoma ellenwelcker, that hairball in the drain, ellenwelcker, that three-year-old is an intertextual act of radical social action she's politeness theory she's a bat poet she's lonely she's a few feet away floating in a sea of plastic debris with a blowhole big enough for a baby to crawl through. O, to throw out your nasty ole ratty ass sweatpants & have a whale swallow them, now this makes me want to die

Ellen Welcker

BLACK PLASTIC NIGHT

Sometimes you're in a bag with a whale and you're naked and furless and this is like Sea World. My fin flopped over like Shamu's, I call with my dying breaths to Ellen. *Ellen*, I whisper, running out of breath, *please please let me out of this bag.* There's no hope for Shamu, she's a goner, but beyond the black plastic I've come to think of as night, the black plastic I've come to think of as my own painted shame, I can hear Ellen shifting, the squeak of her wet suit, the schlop of her scuba shoes. Flippers. I meant flippers. I meant the feet with which you swim. Can Ellen swim like a whale? *ELLL-EN*, I whisper. *I know you can hear me.* Ellen puts down the buck's head she's carrying. She puts down her Ziploc of sparklers. She puts down her makeup bag, her eye shadow, her notebook of diseases. She puts down her cache of cooking utensils. She puts down the giant SUV she shoulders like Jesus. She puts down the soldier she's carrying to the makeshift hospital, the flailing infant, the film of my family. She drops the moon completely. She lets go the string of fish, the bucket of terror. She kneels next to us, right in the middle of the black plastic night. *Maya, dear*, she says, stroking the bag, *there is no way to let you all out. It's like when you're up you're up, and when you're down you're* down—and here, Ellen quotes my children, my children playing the butt game—*But if you like—and think about this before you say yes—I could climb in there with you.* Ellen is crying a little now, and I can hear that she is sorry. Through the black plastic night, I know she is a cache of stars. I can smell the lighter fluid, the burned-down coals of her flaming rock center, the sulphur, the graphite, the metals for writing, the eggy smell of spraying your tomatoes so the deer won't eat them. *Ellen please*, I say, *if you ever loved*—but now Shamu is moving, her skin squeaking a little like a made shoe, and Ellen can't hear me for a moment. My tears—I realize I have been crying too, of course I've been crying—my tears have given Shamu life. *Ellen, if you cry in this bag with me*, I say, *if you cry in this bag, we might be able to help her.* I feel Ellen move closer beside us, tender like a mother. Ellen lassoes a star, really quick, she burns a little hole in the bag, sizzle sizzle, plastic night ripped open to a small blow hole. Ellen puts her lips to the hole, to the whorled shell of my ear. It tickles. *Remember*, Ellen tells me, Ellen tells me like a mother, while the whole world inside the bag strains to listen, *you climbed into that bag all on your own.*

Maya Jewell Zeller

WHAT TO COUNT ON

Not one star, not even the half moon
      on the night you were born
Not the flash of salmon
      nor ridges on blue snow
Not the flicker of raven's
      never-still eye
Not breath frozen in fine hairs
      beading the bull moose's nostril
Not one hand under flannel
      warming before reaching
Not burbot at home under Tanana ice
      not burbot pulled up into failing light
Not the knife blade honed, not the leather sheath
Not raw bawling in the dog yard
      when the musher barks *gee*
Not the gnawed ends of wrist-thick sticks
      mounded over beaver dens
Not solar flares scouring the earth over China
Not rime crystals bearding a sleek cheek of snow
Not six minutes more of darkness each day
Not air water food words touch
Not art
Not anything we expect
Not anything we expect to keep
Not anything we expect to keep us alive

Not the center of the sea
Not the birthplace of the waves
Not the compass too close to true north to guide us

Then with no warning
      flukes of three orcas
            rise, arc clear of sea water

Peggy Shumaker

WE COULD HAVE SAVED THE ORCAS

We could have saved the orcas
but we were so in love with plastic:
straws, beer can holders, and parts for everything,
just so convenient, except when it's time
to be rid of it, just toss it in the ocean,
out of sight, out of mind, and if you need it,
you can sail out to the place in the Pacific
with the floating trash pile, I'm sure
it will be in there somewhere.

We could have saved the orcas
but then we'd all have to take the bus,
get on and sit next to that smelly guy
who's talking about something that happened
in 1983, and who needs that when
you can have a Lexus or at least
a '13 Camry with low miles
that only leaks a little oil.

We could have saved the orcas
but we work so hard, we deserve
a little fun now and then, so let's fly
to Cabo or Machu Picchu, or at least
let's drive to the Grand Canyon,
buy a giant motorhome and save
a ton on motels and meals,
seven miles to the gallon.

We could have saved the orcas
but they eat those Chinook salmon
that taste so good with a little lemon,
so delicious with some corn-on-the-cob
and a nice arugula salad, tofu-dill dressing,
or fresh off the grill, and how much fun

it is to go out on the boat and fish,
pulling in those big ones to gut
and stick in the freezer.

We could have saved the orcas . . .

David M. Laws

CATALOG OF GRIEVANCE

Smoke infiltrates our air, suffocates
the summer.

I water too much or forget altogether, reminded
only by shrivel, by wilt.

An orca scoops her dead calf from the water, nudges
the newborn across

the Salish sea. We call it mourning, but we don't
really know anything

about an orca's inner life. We want to believe
we're privy to this primal

grief, go ahead: add a low moan, a whale
song that might

reverberate in our own sad bones. We have
a list

of grievances against this world, keep
adding items

every day: too hot, too cold, nonsense
in the ether

children blown up, children starved. We want
to lift them

onto our own heads, carry them through our terrible
neighborhoods, hold

their weight for as long as it takes, for as long
as anyone can bear.

Brenda Miller

Salmon Leap

The only constant was the sound of water,
and we, gill-breathing moss
and learning love would be there when we sought her,
prepared ourselves for loss.

Wherever absences are crossed by day
without a touch or look,
whenever there is nothing we can say,
remember the talking brook.

There is no deeper sleep than in the stream,
however it may fall
or heave in tides upon a distant dream.
Whatever voices call,

our ashes will be washed away by rain
and we will speak aloud
the language of a watery refrain,
clear as any cloud.

David Mason

PER NOSTRA CULPA

Blessed be black-bodied
white-patched swimmers
feathering the salty-wet
surface of the Salish Sea
with fluke, flipper and fin.

Blessed be clickers
and whistlers of podsongs,
spouters of rainbow mists,
deep divers, ascenders
bursting into light.

Blessed be tail-slappers,
hunters of Chinook,
chum and sockeye
in depleted and poisoned water,
breachers feasting on free play
even while starving.

Blessed be echolocationists
distracted and derailed
by ship noise,
submarine signals
tour boat motors,
frequency cacophonations
deafening them
to their own voices
and the presence of prey.

Blessed be lifeless residers on beaches.
Blessed be mothers bearing dead children.
Blessed be endangered families with bones
resting on the bottom of the sea.

Through our fault,
through our fault,
through our most grievous fault.

Susan Chase-Foster

Swimming Shiva

We watched them swimming Shiva
In the summer Salish Sea
The baby's lifeless body
Rested on her mother's anguish
Tahlequah's soul torn, her skin a kriah
We glimpsed through the waves.

We watched them swimming Shiva
Seventeen days of grief
The minyan shared the burden
One day for each moon Tahlequah carried
The child in her womb
We heard their mourners' kaddish
A prayer for Tahlequah
A plea to us?

Look! See our circle of sacred sorrow
from your noisy boats and rocky shores
Do you love us, children of the earth?
Will you comfort us, give us Nihum Avelim?
May our memories be for a blessing
You watched us swimming Shiva
Will you sit Shiva for us,
Or inscribe us in the Book of Life?

Glossary of Jewish bereavement terms:

Shiva—Seven days of formal mourning following the burial of a loved one

Kriah—Torn ribbon worn by family as a sign of grief

Minyan—A quorum of Jews necessary for certain prayers and worship

Mourner's Kaddish—The prayer said by and for the bereaved

Nihum Avelim—Respect for the deceased and kindness for those who mourn

Inscribe us in the Book of Life—A common phrase Jewish people say to one another at High Holy Days in the hope we will live to see the next new year.

Julie B. Hunter

EARTH TOTEM

Dorsal cedar dressed in moss where the village stood.
Crest carved fresh and proud, the clan not yet defeated.
White on black the color of starlight, high and old.
Glittering where the sea's back breaks open. In the strait,
their formation ancestors could use to teach children
the ways of courage, certainty, persistence.

Thriving where King Salmon thrive, the throng
charging in their own endemic wave through waves,
splitting the eternal, binding what flows, braiding
salt to salt in a shape the old ones carved in stone,
up from the hidden, forth through the hungry,
diving, secret, swallowed by the sea.

Who will lead us into the future if not these?
Who will teach us high respect, if not
the whales that prey on whales? Who
among us can dance like that, in storm
or cold, driving through shoals of silver
where all the little lives glitter in beautiful fear?

Hold honor of ancestors in our keeping, destiny of children,
eel and clam, eagle and heron, bear and frog, all the woven
hungers nourishing us by their vigor, their abundant life.
How can we meet our children's eager, brimming gaze
if we let the orca essence falter, barren, hungry, gaunt, if
our pod of treasures dive, never to return?

Kim Stafford

I Spot a Fin

I spot a fin fifty yards away, and then a spout. The four smaller fins and more spouting. Jeff fires up the engine and moves the boat closer. Then, in what appears to be a single, choreographed bow, the whales disappear.

We are in perfect position. Jeff shuts off the engine when we hear a massive breath off the bow. My hair stands on end as the entire pod rises mysteriously, like the tide. I sit on the port gunwale when next to me a huge body turns the sea black. The male's dorsal fin passes within inches of my face.

I somehow expect that anything living in the sea must be fishlike, but leaning forward, I see millions of tiny hairs covering the whale's skin. I reach out and touch, mammal to mammal. As his body moves beneath my fingers, I recognize something—brotherhood? And ancient relationship?

Then, without warning, the whale exhales and the air explodes in a magical storm all around me. As I sniff, the watery cloud of his air mixes with my air deep inside my lungs. How familiar his breath smells, like air from a deep, old place, maybe a cave where I lived in another life. In an instant he is gone.

As the pod surfaces again, ten yards away, Jeff maneuvers the boat into position with one hand while holding a Nikon in the other. A female exhales before completely breaking the surface. The surface tension fogs the interface of air and water, enclosing her in a glassy shell. Her six-foot-long baby rolls on his side, never out of touch. I am not aware of the exact moment when the 'killer' part of their name loses its meaning. I no longer feel any fear. The pod inhales and then sinks together, before me one second and gone the next, effortlessly.

The silence while we wait is like the moment between exhale and inhale. Unlike humans, whales have separate passages for food and air, otherwise, they wouldn't be able to feed underwater. Whales breathe through the blowholes on top of their heads, slits surrounded by thick lips of elastic tissue. They open the slit deliberately, and then only to breathe. What must it be like for a whale to stop whatever it's doing every five minutes and rise to the surface to breathe? What does it mean to breathe together as a family?

What if we were aware of *every* breath we took, like whales? What are we missing? What is sweeter than a fresh, entering breath, our bellies rising to contain it, the outer world's life-giving molecules mixing with our bodies? What emotional heights have been reached by animals who are reborn every time they break the ocean's surface to breathe? What does it mean to an individual body to have ancestors who have been breathing together consciously, communally, for millions of years? Is the human imagination supple enough to even consider these questions?

My eye catches the eye of a male. His eye is large, like a glass net float, and reflects the clouds and sky in its smoky surface. A killer whale's eye is set in front of a white patch the size of a football that from a distance might be mistaken for its eye. Our eyes are not so different, the whale's and mine. But what about our minds? Scientists say that the whale's brain is 45 million years old; ours only 2 million. How long before our species evolves enough to reach the humility and peace I feel exists among these whales?

Babies, full of energy, play tag between their lounging parents. One young male nudges his mother, trying to wake her, his pink penis erect and playful. She pushes him away with her tail.

They rub against one another. They purr and sigh. Seldom is one whale not in contact with one or two others. I dream about stripping off my clothes and slipping into the water while they nap, rubbing up against them. I imagine telling Jeff that if something happens, if the whales mistake me for a seal and bite into me, or crush me by accident with their mass, to tell Terry that I always loved her and that I didn't mind dying this way. Even death seems a reasonable price. Some power pulls on me. I want to hold on to a dorsal fin and be pulled through the ocean, to be part of something that from my place on the deck of the *Whaler*, I can barely imagine. One hour is all I want. One hour with my body in constant contact with my fellow mammals, when each of my breaths is part of a family ritual. But I know that this underwater breathless world is not mine. I don't belong.

Brooke Williams

THE POD

dorsal fins up
      for stability
sign of freedom
      in limpid waters
family intact,
      tender connections
belonging
      expansive as oceans
to family and clan
      messages—deep—miles long
will thrive or fail
      in a warming sea.

Carla Shafer

KILLER WHALE SONG

This piece is excerpted from an essay entitled "Lolita: A Killer Whale," which is about the blackfish Lolita, aka Tokitae, captured from Salish Sea resident L Pod back in 1970, and held in a small tank at Miami Seaquarium ever since.

To sing, blackfish blow air through what scientists call *monkey lips*, tissue in the blowhole region of their heads. They can shape the sound that way. Unless they're resting, blackfish talk all the time. Their language consists of clicks, whistles, and pulsed calls. And something we recognize as song.

What we hear as whale song is heard differently by the blackfish. We are creatures of air; they, of water. The medium changes the messaging, if not the message. Individuals are likely known more by how they pattern a song, by their habitual rhythms, than by the thing we know as voice.

The resident blackfish of the Salish Sea have complex social structures. Children will, for the most part, stay with their mothers always. A few matrilines will travel together in a pod; a few pods will form a clan; a few clans will form a community. While they all understand each other, each pod has its own dialect and its own identifying, family song.

Once, an activist took a recording of an L Pod singer to Seaquarium and played it out loud by the side of the pool. Lolita immediately swam over to listen. She trembled. She quivered.

Lolita herself still sings the L Pod family song. Songs are passed from mothers to their children; Lolita learned her song this way, from her mother. She knows where she came from, she knows where she belongs. The song is in her very body, her lungs and monkey lips.

Julie Trimingham

BEREFT, SINGING

All summer my mother has been dying,
a summer of dying Orcas
and skies of smoke.
Bereft offers itself, an old woman wrapped
in the shawl of its etymology—
reft like rift,
a threshold word,
a cleft where the loss seeps in,
salty, diaphanous.

I take the ferry to see my mother
and the Puget Sound, today, is a house of gray,
its upper story freighted with cormorants.
I take up *bereft* like a flashlight
to pick out a path through the dark,
through the gap between life and not-life.

All summer my mother has been dying—
but whose mother, whose child is not dying?

I stand beneath the Osprey's call,
above the Orca's shadow over the deep
and I pass this old word, *bereft,*
from one hand to the other.
Bereft, the heft of it,
the bafflement,
its awful insistence that I sing.

Bethany Reid

ORCAS CALL

When ancestors speak of Earth's life
of deeds, its art and arc of history, they recall
lost identities. Beside the marshes, their drums
warn that harm plus money destroy the harmony

of the mourning doves. They bless the symphony
of crickets, chirp of chickadees, aria of swans.
Beneath this chorus of voices, longings rise,
beloved ones resurrect, and like a child

the poem rushes out the door to
ride with the pod as the orcas call,
to strut and shimmy, sway and dance
in love with words' hypnotic trance.

This poem's small arms lift up the past
for scientists, leaders, artists and readers
men and women of business and crafts
to carry the weight and breath of children.

The orcas call. Poem echoes back:
In the furrows of our brains, memories,
feelings, spirits speak: it's up to us
to plow and plant Earth's internal peace.

Betty Scott

ODE TO AN ORCA

You fling your dolphin body
skyward, breach toward sun
to take a look—sleek, black
and white, aglitter with seawater.
You fluke-wave, roll and flip, sleep
with half a mind, travel miles,
team-hunt, herd chinook, slap
and play. You feed each other.
Your old mother leads the pod,
aids daughter, tends son.
We call you killer whale,
we who kill you with PCBs,
who warm your cold world.
You bond with your pod for life.
You are starving. We dream
of saving what we are killing:
your brainy, love-struck life,
your terrible wild beauty.

Priscilla Long

TAHLEQUAH

This is what a mother will do:
Carry her dead for seventeen days
over one thousand miles balanced
on her own head while the calf
deteriorates in the sun, diving down
to retrieve her each time she slides off
into the water, unable to keep herself
nourished, her own sleek body in danger
of wasting away. This is what we do,
our young part and parcel of our selves,
held in our skin, leaching calcium
from our bones, iron from our blood
as we grow them, as we prepare to say
goodbye. I'm swimming through
these days the best I can, like anyone,
like this orca who'd rather hold her
gone girl than eat the dwindling salmon.
Some say she released her, finally ready
to move on. But I can feel how her
body might have seized when she went
down that last time after the remains,
and there were too few to gather up
again amidst the rush of bubbles.
It won't only be the noise of vessels
that interrupts her feeding now, or how
few fish are jumping in her home
range. Only twenty, and so much loss
already. It may take some time before
she lets herself feel fully hungry again.

Rebecca Hart Olander

WRITING FROM FUTURE MEMORY

It was something I couldn't anticipate. At one moment, there was water, seemingly endless off the starboard side of the boat. I was braced against the stern, my thighs pressed for balance. Waves rocked the tiny vessel mercilessly. I scanned the water hundreds of yards away and, closer, noticed two people in a small dinghy, one with an almost-comic telescopic lens on an expensive camera.

It was the summer of 1995, just before my senior year of high school. We'd just returned from our annual trip to the Oregon Coast and had taken a campus tour at the University of Oregon. I'd made up my mind; I wanted to study English there after I graduated.

But in the back of the boat, everything changed.

The spray of watery breath hit me, and I inhaled. For a moment, we were bound by air, water, life. An orca from J Pod had just surfaced next to me. The boat kept bobbing. I heard ecstatic screams. Cameras clacked as users advanced film. The telescopic lens couldn't focus on what had come so close. Then, the black and white disappeared underwater as quickly as it arrived. The superpod of the J, K, and L Pods moved on.

We couldn't believe it. Our first time whale watching in the San Juans. Our first time with orcas. We'd seen gray whales in Oregon, but gray whales were boring, sluggish. The most exciting aspects were my young brother's cries about sharks in the water.

Back on land, we sped from the docks in Friday Harbor to the cliffs on the south side of San Juan Island. For hours, we sat on the mossy rocks and watched the open expanses of water. This was orca territory, and visitors often spotted them offshore. Soon, watery breaths, a repeated *whoosh* that filled the chest with anticipation and wonder. Then, the tell-tale dorsal fins in the distance.

I abandoned being a writer. Now, marine biology, researching the Southern Residents. During senior year, I dreamed about the whales while I excelled in English, looking forward to college classes in my new field.

When my admission to UO fell through, I was devastated. At my local community college, I took vertebrate zoology twice. These were signs I took to heart, and I got back on track, finishing my Bachelors in English at the University of Washington. Living in Seattle allowed easy access to the islands for day trips, weekends, retreats.

After years away from the northwest, I'm now back in Seattle. I visited the islands this spring, but too early for whales. With the significant decline in the J, K, and L populations, I know that each visit, each sighting is precious, incalculable. I understand my role as writer, teacher, visitor. With each patient watch, each joyous anticipation before the *whoosh* of breath, I build a memory to pass on. A feeling of completeness. Because one day, I might sit on the cliffs, trying to remember a sound that is gone.

Jenne Knight

No Wake

I rowed the dinghy backward, floating slow above deep red urchins, bright orange starfish, blue-grey abalone gripping coral-pink rocks. From this angle the sea was transparent, its technicolor contents naked to my presence. Small fish zippered away from my oars.

eel grass
at low tide
unpinned hair
across a pillow

Attached to beams in the wharf above: stacked and flattened balls of mud resembled very closely pots of a small-handed tribe. If I stood in the dinghy at high tide, I could almost see the eggs inside. Hear peeping.

long-tailed
barn swallow
quick scissors
follow

Nancy Pagh

ASCENDANCE

After a historic photograph by Ellis Morigeau

When a wild chinook thrashes the air
above Kettle Falls,
the coiled spring of its body
ripples with the surge of 700 river miles
                        toward home.

The river pours its thunder
between striate seabottom rocks:
a glassy tongue imploding into whiteness.

To the salmon it is a beckoning arm.

There is no human gesture so fervent
—this long journey inland—
no effort so seamlessly one with its element.

The river's story, descending
through epochs of ice and stone,
coalesces in the salmon's momentary flight.

The salmon's heart
is the river's heart made flesh.
The salmon's flight, a pulse.

Ours is the wisdom to see them both
as one; power to power joined:

one falling,
one borne by a wisdom all its own

            in ascendance.

Tim McNulty

WHAT I KNOW ABOUT ORCAS

When I told my husband I was writing about Southern Resident orcas, he said, "You don't know anything about orcas." I bristled, and snapped back, "Yes I do!" After a walk and soul-searching, I came to uncomfortable conclusions.

One.
What I know about orcas I could pour into a teacup. And still have room for cream. What I know most is the idea of them. Stiff jut of dorsal fin, angel-wing shape of a fluke, black and white puzzle pieces of a body. I live on the edge of the Salish Sea so I can't help but know about the existence of the Southern Resident pods. I've seen glimpses of sleek orca bodies from the deck of a ferry and felt awe. I've looked down from a tiny San Juan Island bound commuter plane and seen orca fins splitting the sea, the white foam of their watery contrails. I've felt a bubbling up of joy.

Two.
Some of what I know about orcas I've folded into the palm of my hand like a coin in a disappearing magic trick. I know about the dwindling salmon, disruptive sonic assaults of vessels, the oceanic toxics. But while a ferry rumbled through and a little plane flew over the orca-animated sea, I managed to take in only my excitement and joy at seeing those beautiful and graceful beings. As if the signs that they are losing food, strength, health, habitat, and their very future disappeared from my sight. Then I watched, along with countless others, Tahlequah's heartbreaking seventeen-day vigil for her dead newborn. I couldn't turn away from her grief. I could taste it. It tasted like the long drink of goodbye.

Three.
What I truly know about orcas, after the tea leaves have settled at the bottom of my cup, after I've opened my hand to expose the coin I've been avoiding, is that the orcas are starving and struggling and disappearing and I am heartbroken. And I am complicit. That is a tough conclusion for me, a person who tends a wildlife-friendly garden, who cares about the environment. A person who loves orcas. They have given me awe and joy. I have given them nothing. Worse than nothing. Who knows how I may have harmed them already by small careless acts and by not speaking out?

I have no way to know whether I can make any difference at all to the survival of resident orcas. But I have to hold out hope for them. And I have to do something. Learn more. Donate money. Donate time. Change habits. Change policy. Maybe the reviving elixir for the orcas will be made up of science, public policy, corporate restraint, and the small acts and voices of individuals who choose to try. Maybe me. Maybe you. Maybe there is still time. Meanwhile, we can start by stopping our part in serving the surviving orcas their last long drink of goodbye.

Victoria Doerper

ECLIPSED

Out of the ocean.
Mother lifts limp half-moon
   young.
The grief goes on
   for days.

How we celebrated the passing shadow
   across the sun, yet we neglect

generations of
yin-yang bodies that
arc and sing.

Mysterious tides reflecting sky.

Our sea, now a cauldron of loss
   and plastic.
Our collective future,
   a hazy regret.

Jessica Gigot

Earth to Earth

When bigleaf maple leaves larger than your face turn yellow with bronze fungal spots, it is time. When the lackadaisical songbirds of late summer join in fervent, chittering mixed-species flocks, trembling the cedars, it is time. When rains return and licorice ferns green and unfurl, and mushrooms of muted reds and purples appear out of dead wood, it is time.

They are coming home, to die.

I come to the river to watch. A silver streak in the pebbled shallows, a crimson flash that seems a trick of the eye, or the water. But no—a fin there. A whitewater tail swish, just there. Chinook salmon returning from the Pacific Ocean to spawn.

One September morning I stood, not on a riverbank, but next to a rectangular tank holding a writhing swarm of Clackamas River Chinook. I pulled rain gear and galoshes over my park ranger uniform and awaited instructions from the hatchery technicians.

You want me to do what??

I reached into the steel box of river water and slid a hand along a spotted, coppery-red body longer than my arm, then squinted as his tail lashed water at my face. The deep white gash adorning his side reminded me he was one of only two or three of his parents' 3,000+ eggs that had survived not just to adulthood, but a thousands-miles journey, six years in the open ocean, then back up three rivers home again. *Oh the places you've been.*

I grabbed tight, with both hands—one around his thrashing tail, the other gripping his slippery belly—and pulled the gasping fish from the water. He whipped his head and tail and just as quickly snapped back the other direction. Fearing I would drop him, I kneeled and bear-hugged his fifty-pounds to my chest, then stood, arms erect, and placed his nose in a notched pedestal. One of the technicians raised a metal baseball bat and brought it down, thunk, on his head. The salmon went limp.

They come home to die.

Not this death, I knew, but the still rapid and no less violent death that comes from a journey so arduous it literally takes the life out of a body no longer acclimatized to fresh water, physically beaten, starving, and which—if it hasn't already become prey—dies within days after spawning. Because that is the natural cycle. Life begets life.

I told myself this as I joked with the technicians and tried to pretend my hands weren't shaking. At the end of the day after I'd showered but still stank, when I still shook, I realized these weren't the tremors of discomfort from helping kill fish.

I was giddy.

I was electrified by my intimacy with the mighty Chinook in that moment when life becomes death. An intimacy no books, experts, or naturalist training could ever teach. The intimacy of death, like sex, is to know an other in the deepest, most visceral sense. Hunters know this.

Many of the fish I helped kill that day had their eggs or sperm harvested to make more hatchery salmon, then they went on to feed people. Others were trucked back to the open river and left to rot, to feed everything else. Though we may be greedy animals who take more than our share, we are learning, or maybe, remembering. Remembering that no lives are lived in isolation. That some lives reach farther than others and continue rippling outward even in death.

Spawning salmon do more than pass on DNA. Their carcasses bring nutrients like nitrogen, carbon, sulfur and phosphorous that fertilize riverside plants and feed insect larvae. They in turn support entire rivers, including juvenile salmon. All of which nourishes forests far from rivers, down to mushrooms on cedars thick with insectivorous songbirds. Death begets life.

Mary Oliver asks us, in "The Summer Day": *What is it you plan to do with your one wild and precious life?* I ask, on a fall day, what might we do after that?

If I could, I would not seal myself in a box, nor burn my body to ashes and dust. If I could, I would give my self to the river, to be torn apart by eagles and bears, to be nibbled by fingerlings. Soaked up by cedars or washed out to sea. To discover a new slant on intimacy.

Heather Durham

ANOTHER STRAND

A few years ago, I took a long walk up a cold stream and learned a lesson in reverence. I'd been trying to write about endangered salmon and realized I knew nothing about them, so I called the Forest Service, and next thing you know I stood at a trailhead with waders in my pack and a broomstick in my hand.

The crew leader, Cindy, and I dropped down through clumps of head-high devil's club. Patches of sunlight set yellow cottonwood leaves and dew-wet moss a shimmer. As we walked, Cindy explained these surveys, which she'd been doing for twenty years—twenty!—and gave me a primer on salmon spawning preferences. They want the coldest cleanest water, the least manipulated stream banks, the most intact forests.

When we reached the main tributary, Cindy forged ahead. The rocks on the bottom ranged from rust to orange, with quartz veins shimmering white. Where the rocks were polished clean—no dirt, no algae—that's where we looked. There, the fish dig a shallow depression, lay eggs, then cover them with rocks the size of a toddler's fist: the redd. After an hour or so, I began to see redds clearly. We'd hang a flag on a nearby limb and label them: possible, probable, definite.

Suddenly, Cindy stopped.

A spawning pair!

In a shallow eddy, the male eased beside the female, more snuggle than thrust, and the female flipped on her back and writhed. What part of the sex act, I wondered, was this?

"She's working," Cindy said. "That's how she cleans the rocks."

On cue, the male joined the frenzy, and together they did a little housework.

Cindy stood watching, beaming in silence.

Back home when I'd try to describe the scene in the creek—like prayer, I'd say—I'd picture Cindy, too.

We know what happens to the salmon in this mountain stream affects what happens to orcas in the Salish Sea. They're connected by a string of complex ecological systems from water temperature to insect populations to sea lions lurking hungrily on shore, and threatened by a string of equally familiar industrial ones, from the seven major dams on the

Columbia River between here and the Pacific, to shade-stripping logging operations, and finally the fisherman, and all of us, browsing cellophane-wrapped packages at QFC.

But there's another strand in the weave: people all over the Pacific Northwest who devote themselves to the everyday work of caring, from monitoring streams to building fish passages at dams to installing road culverts and restoring vegetation on stream banks. It's unglamorous work usually—meetings, meetings, and more meetings—and it's sometimes disheartening, but they do it out of conscience and commitment, and something more, too: a deep reverence, which they've quietly nurtured like long love—for ten years, twenty, and more—so every single time they see salmon spawn or orcas breach, they watch in awe.

Ana Maria Spagna

THE YEAR-KING'S SACRIFICE

I have this vase
on which the salmon writhe
in wild profusion.
Every line of their carven
carving bodies signals
forward.
So many
the artist barely imaged
the waters they've shoved aside.

The only time
I saw this many living,
they were dying.
Every line of their silver
slivered bodies blurring
to forest.
Lives spent
in giving their own to life,
they gave up—broken for you.

Broken for all
—the stench of which is bracing.
Holds us up.
Their wild deaths
our pulsing, wild life.

Tara K. Shepersky

IN THE TLINGIT LANGUAGE

In the Tlingit language, the word for killer-whale, *keet*, means "supernatural being." We'll never know its true connection, but it fits. In nature, creatures defy our assumptions. In the 1980s, biologists divided fish-eating killer-whales into pods, extended family groups that remained together for life. Recently, that story has been revised. These societies orbit around the matriline, mothers and offspring. Pods can fracture. The loss of a key female may cause a family to rupture, for bonds to loosen. Discoveries reveal the *keet* nature of the wild animal. And the more we know, the longer we stay, the more we care, and caring, like anthropomorphism, is tricky ground for that detached creature, the scientist.

For the past few years, we've been collecting samples from killer whales to measure contaminant levels in their blubber, to extract DNA from their skin. We've learned that their populations are small, a few hundred animals, so an oil spill or a die-off of salmon or seals can be catastrophic. We've confirmed that residents and transients don't interbreed, though they share the same waters, that transients carry high PCB and DDT levels in their blubber, that mothers pass these poisons to calves through their milk. But to learn this, we have to approach whales more closely than we do to take photographs. To do this, we point a rifle at a whale and shoot a biopsy dart into its body. The dart pops out after snagging an inch-long piece of flesh on its thread-like barb, and we scoop it from the water with a dip net. To do this, Craig and I argue through our conflicted feelings. *We can't dart now; they're resting. These animals are rare. We can't dart in front of tour boats. We might not have another chance. We've probably darted enough animals in this group. We need more samples for the statistical tests. We have to have a common mind. I hate all this.*

Even Lars, who's enthusiastic about shooting, scrunches down in the bow, fingers plugged in his ears, eyes shut tight when the shot's fired.

Eva Saulitis

129

Dio

His name is Dio. Friends sometimes call him Ronnie James.

"Why is that?" I ask my host, Deborah Giles, research scientist with University of Washington's (UW) Center for Conservation Biology. "Black Sabbath," Giles replies, her matter-of-fact tone reminding me I know nothing about heavy metal—though as I peek at the scrappy little cattle dog peering back at me from within his crate, I can intuitively see how he'd evoke a metalhead persona.

Dio emits a high-pitched whine, as if in deference to the singer after whom he was named. I later learn that Ronnie James, the man, was known for his high falsetto. But Dio the dog's talent lies more in his nose than his vocal chords. Since the 1990s, scat detection dogs like Dio have been helping scientists bridge the olfaction gap between humans and canines. These energetic, eager-to-please mutts—often rescued from shelters—use their remarkable sense of smell to find wildlife feces, which in turn speak tomes about animal health and genetics.

"We can get a huge amount of information about all of the major threats to orcas, and we do it noninvasively, which is even better," says Giles, who has been working with UW's Conservation Canines (CK9) program since 2009. The program is led by Dr. Samuel Wasser, the Center's director and scientific pioneer of the scat detection dog method. Dog-detected orca scats have enabled Wasser's lab to evaluate the effects of inadequate prey, vessel traffic, and toxic contaminants on the Southern Resident population.

This late August afternoon, I'm accompanying Giles, Dio, and CK9 handlers Collette Yee and Mairi Poisson on a training session off San Juan Island. Yee is lead handler on the orca project, while Poisson is being prepped as a back-up for the future.

Scat detection at sea takes teamwork and patience. With Giles at the helm, Dio stands perched like a sentinel on the bow of Wasser's 21-foot Grady-White—Poisson stationed directly beside him. Yee is situated nearby to help interpret Dio's behavior. Giles slowly trolls transect lines perpendicular to the breeze and waits for the boat to enter the "scent cone" emanating from the scat sample—a small plastic bowl containing liquidy whale poop and dropped over the side during an earlier drive-by. Handlers must scrutinize the dog's body language from head to tail to search for subtle cues indicating he might be onto a scent. If Dio's actions become more animated, Poisson will direct Giles to steer into the wind so they can make their way toward the source. All three women will keep watching Dio carefully, reading his hot or cold movements to adjust their course as needed.

Yee explains what she looks for in Dio's behavior: elevated nose, tongue licking at the air, a certain je-ne-sais-quoi expression on his face. Sometimes he gets excited about the waves lapping at the boat or a gull flying overhead; you've got to know your dog, says Yee. And since Dio doesn't have a tail, she reminds us, you can only discern a wiggle.

CK9 teams have been invaluable to the urgent pursuit of knowledge about the orcas' plight. Between 2007 and 2014, they collected 348 scat samples from 79 Southern Residents—samples that have since unlocked invaluable information about the reproductive woes of females. Analyses of hormones contained in the scats revealed a 69% pregnancy failure rate.

Recent images of J35 carrying her deceased calf around Puget Sound for 17 days have brought these frightening statistics to life—and a mother's grief is a potent portal. With all the world watching, J35 would not let us forget that her loss is a harbinger of things to come unless we figure out a way to restore vital Chinook to her family's diet.

Back on the water, Dio senses change in the air. He casts his twitching nose skyward and begins to pace as we enter the scent cone. Poisson signals Giles, who's already turning into the wind. Dio leans over the edge of the bow, nose now pointing ahead like the needle of a compass, elbows resting against the fiberglass hull as he anticipates his reward. Minutes later, Poisson reaches into the Sound and picks up the little blue bowl. She hands the bowl to Giles, who swiftly passes it in front of the wiggling Dio while the team bellows "Good bu-oy! Good bu-oy!" A happy, once-homeless cattle dog plays with a bright green plastic ball, and at least for the moment, our hearts sing like there's no tomorrow.

Paula MacKay

BETWEEN HIGHWAY 2 AND THE WENATCHEE

Splashes pulled me over and down
to the sand. What looked from the car
like boiling in the river was a collective shudder,
thrash of fin and sporadic scale.

With a clatter of rocks, a couple
clad in camouflage appears. "Fall run," I say.
He nods and glasses a wet smack
where one buck drives off another.
"Men!" she says and winks.
He wears a cowboy hat over a dark moustache.
Her curves press against her landscape,
ample cleavage in a V of leaf shapes. "Anadromous,"
I say, for the mere feel of the word
for breathing two worlds. Another hen
lashes herself against the gravel.

Bear tracks led them here. "You can get two a year,"
he says, "one for each side of the mountains."
They're here for their second.
"Seen any?"

And a black bear emerges
again from the brush behind my house,
flaring her long ears and crinkling her snout
during slow seconds
while two cubs, with clumsy shuffles
through stems and leaves, appear.
My wife holds our daughter
as I offer the soft growl of a new word.
The mother's fur nearly blond,
the cubs swinging dark heads, snuffing.

"Sorry," I say, shaking my head.
She says, "You can use anything,
black powder, a bow—you can even shoot the cubs
but nobody does."

"Still enough light to bag a bear,"
he says, and they turn
and vanish through leaves.

Derek Sheffield

Rain Gardens for Whales, Salmon, and Clean Water

I scrape coho salmon skin and bones into my kitchen's compost pail and think of J50. She died ill, probably starving, her young body falling through Puget Sound's polluted waters until coming to rest on the seabed. Scavengers will eat her skin; marine invertebrates will colonize her bones. J50 will feed a host of creatures and support a food chain that might include the salmon I'll eat. Something similar happens on land, where old trees fall to the ground and become nurse logs that restore nutrients to the soil and provide habitat for salal, salmonberry, Douglas fir, and other native flora that capture rain and seep it into a welcoming earth where it drains to waterways as cool, clean groundwater.

But rain also falls on roads, sidewalks, and other impervious surfaces where it picks up car oil, pet waste, pesticides, fertilizers, soaps, and just about anything else. Rain becomes stormwater runoff pouring into the rivers and streams that flow into Puget Sound. Caught in the flow (or arriving from other sources) are persistent organic pollutants (POPs), especially PDBEs, dioxins, and PCBs that become stored in the fatty deposits of salmon and other fish, and the predators that eat them. As long-lived predators, orcas accumulate high levels of PCBs and other toxins in their blubber, which are released when females nurse their young, or adults draw on fat reserves due to hunger. Closer to home, I've seen coho enter Seattle's Longfellow Creek ready to spawn only to die before finding a mate due to stormwater runoff, a phenomenon happening across our region's urban and suburban streams.

I yank the compostable bag out of the pail, open the back door, and toss food scraps into the yard waste bin. September rain drizzles my face. Winter after winter, runoff has poured down our driveway, across the carport, over the walkway, under the back door, and into the basement. Finally, the landlord lowered the walkway drain; runoff flows into an underground tank, which I worry drains down the alley, through a sewer grate, and eventually into Puget Sound.

A genuine solution is my neighbor's rain garden, which seeps runoff through layers of compost, gravel, soil, and mulch held in place by cedars, sword fern, and other native plants. Pour stormwater through these basic components of a rain garden, and studies prove toxins are sufficiently filtered out that coho survive. The average rain garden filters an estimated 30,000 gallons (600 filled bathtubs) of water annually. Rain gardens, cisterns, and other green stormwater infrastructure are simple ways that businesses, schools, community centers, and homeowners can reduce the runoff reaching Puget Sound.

I close the bin and head inside. There are so many hard tasks ahead: take down dams; restore Chinook runs; manage vessel traffic. Then there's the joy of creating a garden for clean water, salmon, and whales.

Adrienne Ross Scanlan

SEEING ORCA

To see an orca you must see the waters it hunts in. To see the waters it hunts in you must see the land the waters nuzzle, where the salmon come down the rivers. To see the salmon come down the rivers you must see the streams that spawn them. As your eyes climb you realize, to see one of our Southern Resident orcas you must look as high as mountains.

That is where our betrayal began, up there, among the peaks shedding rain and snowmelt. In the early 1900s we began strangling their rivers with dams: dams for irrigation, dams for hydroelectric, and in the case of the lower four on the Snake River, dams to create a massive loch system for barging wheat down to the Columbia River and out to market. We dammed streams too. We dammed about whatever we could during the dam building heyday. If you want to know why our orcas are starving, it's largely because we killed their ancient salmon runs with dams.

With so many dams, four thousand by some estimates, why so much focus on the Snake's lower four? One word: Chinook. Chinook, or "Kings," are the largest of the salmon, allowing orca to gain more meal per hunt, thus conserving critical energy. For our orcas, Chinook are bread and butter, 80% of their diet, and the Snake River, a major tributary to the Columbia, once produced some of the largest Chinook runs in the world.

Shaped like a ladle, the Snake cups the eastward bulge of the Rocky Mountains in Montana and Idaho, gathering vast flows of cool, mineral laden water and sending it, along with drainage from the Columbian plateau, northwest through Hells Canyon and across the loess of Washington, before emptying into the Columbia. As late as the 1930s, even after ten dams had been built on the upper reaches, fall Chinook runs of half a million were coursing upstream each spring. But then, beginning in the 1960s, the US Army Corps of Engineers built the lower four, and by the 1980s only 78 wild Chinook made it as far as Lower Granite Dam, the fourth up the chain.

What a shame. Just above it sprawls a vast watershed of prime Chinook spawning habitat, with 5,000 miles of streams and rivers, mostly preserved as wilderness and still in a pristine state. It is a Chinook Valhalla, and the only thing standing in the way of it and the orcas are the lower four dams. Breach them, and you feed the orcas. It's that simple.

Of course, as soon you consider the communities that grew up around the dams, simple becomes complex again. Real people with diverse livelihoods are connected to those dams, and any agreement needs to account for them, with compensation and retraining for those directly affected. But the cup that is emptied is also filled, by a globally significant restoration project which will bring students, researchers, fishers, nature lovers, hikers, kayakers, honeymooners, retirees, lone adventurers, vacationing families, and their pocketbooks from around the world.

I'm sure when they built those dams no one imagined a grieving orca mother one day carrying her dead calf seventeen days through the sea in a near-mythic tour of maternal grief. But she has. And we have seen, and if the seeing didn't change us, it should have. If we can't uncurl our grip now, let loose this final, obvious stretch of this one river, we are functionally set in our own cement.

We have dammed even ourselves.

Rob Lewis

IT'S NOT WATCHING

If you grew up in the middle of the country, the idea of being on a boat in the Pacific Ocean seeing a whale was about as exotic as you could imagine.

Several years after my husband and I and our children moved to Los Angeles and the girls were a little older, we promised them that we would go whale watching. We waited for my parents to join us—they were landlocked in Missouri. A month before the trip the girls and I read every book we could find on orcas and whales in the children's section of the Santa Monica library. I remember reading *The Happy Little Whale*, a Little Golden Book, until I knew it by heart.

The day we boarded the boat in San Pedro harbor was not what I had imagined. It was gray, overcast and actually chilly. We spent hours going from the deck to the cabin to warm up; by three in the afternoon we were hoping to see almost anything. Suddenly, hot chocolate spilling over the edges of our paper cups, the boat took off and the captain announced whales had been spotted. We clambered up to the deck, hung on to the railing, and searched the horizon with our tired eyes.

There in a fair distance from the boat we saw them—several whales. The boat sped up and got as close as the captain said was proper as we watched them do their thing—rolling, dipping, rising, spouting as though for our private showing. The passengers were silent and in the word we throw around now like confetti, back then it was truly awesome.

While I admit to not having great sea legs, I felt unsettled in a way I couldn't describe and certainly didn't want to mention. The excitement on the faces of my kids was reward enough for a long day that left me wondering. Back home and all of us into dry, warm clothes I pulled out a roll of butcher paper and assigned the six of us to draw what we liked the best about the day. As I remember, my father drew the vast ocean he'd never seen before; my mother drew our girls. Our daughters drew their versions of the whales in the water. My husband did his best of whales spouting and I, the better artist of the adults, couldn't get into my own bright idea. I drew all of us in stick figures at the dock waiting to board.

That was the only time we whale watched and now forty years later I understand why I never wanted to go again. It's not whale watching—it's hunting. You can soften the activity with a euphemism like we do for other activities—collateral damage comes to mind. But, call it what you will, it's hunting and now it's almost too late to do even that. We seem to be able to wreck almost everything we start out loving—birds, mammals, whales, orcas—the list is enormous and keeps growing. I'm not a scientist. I'm just a woman who knew even while the sea air was whipping her hair around on the boat that it wasn't watching.

Barbara Clarke

My River

It flows quietly past our small towns
like most rivers civilized long ago,
my river, the Puyallup. Hard to pronounce,
levied to tame it, fished only by treaty
or license, it is where I follow when I need
a river to take me back to place remote,
where I might know what was lost
when its name was first spoken from a map.

It is not mighty. It is not of any fame.
It works no wonders of flood or heartache.
No literature or song tells of romance
along its banks. It is found on no global map.
To speak it anywhere east of its mountain
requires humility when so few know of it.

But it is my Mississippi, my Congo, my Nile,
my Yangtze, my Amazon—any great river
one might name. Yes, levies. Yes, bridges.
Yes, fences along its banks, A diversion dam
and a flume using its water for electricity.
Changes of course man-made into Tacoma.

But up past the power plant at Electron,
into the foothills, finally in the deep woods
of the national park, I stand hoping to hear
in the sound of the untamed water over boulders
and tree roots what the Puyallups
and Nisquallys and the Nooksacks heard along
their rivers coming out of their mountains
down to the salt water of the Puget Sound.

Tim Sherry

RECORD SALMON RUN

In the depths, I glimpse them,
grey shadows that flicker
or rest under the log bridge:
a kind of effortless hovering
(gills open and close)
in the circular act of breathing.

Then turning flint faces,
they muscle their way up,
Silver scales glinting in sunlight.
Agony of sheer will, sheer toil,
flounder up fall, or flip—
      a moment's flight broken
by rocks
           tossed
               in roiling waters,
gashed
               on sharp snags.
I wonder how they go
without eating,
leave the ocean
without hope of return,
die without
seeing their young,
follow the magnetic pull
of home.

Christen Mattix

141

A Prayer for Holding

To be a body that resembles what holds it is to be closer to God
than man. To be an orca — skin smooth as water — is to be both

embrace & what is held within. Some days I worry I don't know
how to fit in with this earth, & then, turning my body into the arms

of another, I sleep easy, full of dreams. But most days I long to be
water. I am thinking of Tahlequah, the mother whale who carried

the burden of her dead calf for over a thousand miles. I don't like
how, not resembling God, I have been a part of a history that destroys

all that does, a history that kills too much of what it does not know
simply because it does not know it, & then refuses to call this genocide.

At SeaWorld, orcas—made angry by captivity—bit skin off each other,
which the workers took home as souvenirs. Show me how this is not a new

story, how man has made of all who are not man a fear of being themselves.
& so the orca, ripping the skin off the other orca. Like a star veiling another

star, as if to say: no one sits below to read by your light. I miss the world
we never had because we missed that world. How we held it & how we let it fall.

Oh God. I know you don't resemble me, & so I ask: if, wanting solitude,
we offered solitude, would that be alright? If, wanting love, we offered love,

would that be alright? If, holding all we hold the way we are held by air—
which is to say with a kind of tenderness that forgives our breath before

we breathe—which is to say the way a mother would, carrying her child
a thousand miles—which is to say so close to being, but not exactly, inhuman—

would that be alright?

Devin Gael Kelly

LEARNING TO KEEN.

In one photograph he is wave-tossed, sun-bleached, bright against the dark rocks of Kalaloch, Copalis, Vashon, or Lopez.

In another, he wears a sweatshirt—light blue with white letters "Camp Orkila."

In a third we stand small against the sky, hands clasped, hair tangled together. We wear t-shirts "Save the Whales!" an imperative the world did not hear.

We do not name the dead or if we do, in half-remembered whispers, in ill-wrought elegies or indie-rock lyrics.

He is long lost in waves and time, his bones and body become ash scattered across mountains, rivers, oceans.

I sleep seldom and then on a storm-tossed dream sea filled with the shadows of Salish, with the curving arcs of Orca, with a bone-deep keen.

We are told there is no future, no hope, that we are beyond redemption. I stand here, as I have always done, hands clasped at the edge of the world, refusing to submit.

Yvonne Garrett

RITE

Call them by the harsh name,
      killers,

lethal cylinders
      fast as submarines,

apex predators of the sea
      as we are on the land.

Sociable in groups, like us,
      big-brained,

organized
      joyous hunters,

they impale their prey
      with conical teeth

the way the black-and-white
      loggerhead shrike

kills on a fence barb
      or thorn of the acacia.

The transient pod encircles
      a cornered whale

as if water
      is a tightrope,

a blood dance
      we ourselves have dreamed.

FOR LOVE OF ORCAS

Children in delight or horror
>   are brought to see

the captive ones perform
>   an acrobatic ruination,

or, luckier, may watch from boats
>   a resident mother

defend her single calf,
>   or mourn it, carrying grief

for days on end
>   across the Sound,

repeatedly nudging the dead one
>   to swim again.

We risk ourselves by ignoring
>   their dangerous beauty,

their shared mammalian cunning,
>   they way they speak

our ancient will
>   not to disappear.

Stan Sanvel Rubin

THE HONOURED DEAD

Here lies one whose name was writ in water.

—John Keats

KwiTahlequah, Daughter of Tahlequah, was born July 24, 2018 and died less than an hour later. She was the seventy-third Southern Resident (that humans are aware of) lost since 1998. Her body was carried by her mother for 17 days as another member of J Pod wasted away. Days later Scarlet joined her—dropping the critically endangered population even more.

Memorials around the world list the names of the honoured dead. Never forget...

Scarlet (2014-2018) the miracle baby delivered by a breach birth in 2014 to Slick. The flying baby orca and symbol of the baby boom was declared missing July 13th. J50.

KwiTahlequah (2018-2018). Daughter of Tahlequah. She would have been J56. I think she should be designated J56 so her life and death never disappear from the scientific records.

Crewser (1995-2018) son of Rascal. L92.

Sonic (2015-2017), son of Rascal. J52.

Skagit (1972-2017), daughter of K Pod. K13.

Granny (1911-2017) beloved matriarch of the Salish Sea. J2.

Doublestuf (1998-2016) son of Oreo. J34.

Dipper (2015-2016) son of Polaris. J54.

Polaris (1993-2016) daughter of Princess Angeline. J28.

Samish (1974-2016) daughter of Sissy. J14.

Nigel (1996-2016) son of Jellyroll. L95.

J55 (2016-2016) child of J Pod. J55.

Ophelia (1965-2015) daughter of L Pod. L27.

Rhapsody (1996-2014) daughter of Ewok. J32.

L120 (Sept. 2014-Oct. 2014) child of Surprise! L120.

Lulu (1977-2014) daughter of Canuck. L53.

Indigo (2001-2014) son of Ino. L100.

Speiden (1933-2013) daughter of J Pod. J8.

Skana (1979-2013) son of Spirit. L79.

Grace (1960-2012) daughter of L Pod. L2.

Baba (1956-2013) daughter of L Pod. L26.

Gaia (1989-2012) son of Grace. L78.

Raggedy (1963-2012) daughter of Kiska. K40.

Tanya (1964-2012) daughter of L Pod. L5.

Alexis (1933-2012) daughter of L Pod. L12.

Riptide (1996-2012) son of Samish. J30.

Victoria/Sooke (2009-2012) daughter of Surprise! L112.

J48 (Dec 2011-Jan 2012) child of Slick. J48.

Ruffles (1951-2010) son of Granny. J1.

Canuck (1961-2010) daughter of L Pod. L7.

Keet (1996-2010) son of Slick. J33.

Georgia (1933-2010) daughter of K Pod. K11.

L114 (2010-2010) child of Matia. L114.

Flash (1986-2010) son of Tanya. L73.

Saanich (1986-2010) son of Oreana. L74.

Faith (1977-2008) son of Asterix. L57.

Splash (1985-2008) daughter of Grace. L67.

L111 (2008-2008) daughter of Marina. L111.

Blossom (1972-2008) daughter of Mama. J11.

Ankh (1950-2008) daughter of L Pod. L21.

Aurora (2002-2008) daughter of Splash. L101.

Lummi (1910-2008) daughter of K Pod. K7.

J43 (2007-2008) child of Samish. J43.

L104 (2004-2007) child of Jelly Roll. L104.

K41 (2006-2006) child of Sekiu. K41.

K39 (Sept. 2006-Oct. 2006) child of Raven. K39.

Raven (1994-2006) daughter of Sequim. K28.

Jellyroll (1972-2006) daughter of L Pod. L43.

Hugo (1986-2006) son of Baba. L71.

Luna (1999-2006) son of Splash. The world famous orca was separated from his pod and joined humans in Nootka Sound. The Mowachaht/Muchalaht people say he held the soul of their newly dead chief, Ambrose. Killed by a tugboat driver. L98.

Tatoosh (1999-2006) son of Sequim. K31.

Olympia (1955-2005) daughter of L Pod. L32.

L107 (2005-2005) child of Marina. L107.

Kiska (1948-2003) daughter of K Pod. K18.

Sparky (1980-2003) son of Tanya. L58.

Oreana (1950-2002) daughter of L Pod. L3.

L102 (2002-2002) child of Marina. L102.

Rascal (1972-2002) daughter of L Pod. L60.

K32 (2000-2001) child of Opus. K32.

L99 (2000-2001) daughter of Marina. L99.

Cetus (1980-2000) son of Ophelia. L62.

Orcan (1975-2000) son of Grace. L39.

Squirty (1957-2000) daughter of L Pod. L11.

Oskar (1959-2000) son of L Pod. L1.

Everett (1977-2000) son of Tahoma. J18.

Tahoma (1962-1999) daughter of J Pod. J10.

Morgan (1933-1999) daughter of K Pod. K4.

L97 (1999-1999) child of Nootka. L97.

Nootka (1973-1999) daughter of L Pod. L51.

J11's Calf (1998-1998) child of Blossom.

Nerka (1995-1998) daughter of Ophelia. L93.

Dylan (1965-1998) son of L Pod. L38.

Leo (1974-1998) son of Olympia. L44.

Sounder (1954-1998) daughter of K Pod. K3.

Ewok (1981-1998) daughter of Tahoma. J20.

Note: Information for the above list is drawn from research available from The Center for Whale Research (whaleresearch.com) and Orca Net (orcanet.org).

Mark Leiren-Young

SEA CHANGE

After Da-ka-xeen Mehner's sculpture, Weapon of Oil

Solar wind takes two days
        to reach us,
oval aurora throbbing, sun
        more agitated
this year than last.

        Ice walkers see
through the thinning pack
        seal shadows gliding.
Daggers of oil slip
        between our ribs.

        We have some serious
vanishing to do.

Peggy Shumaker

WHALES

In the mountain's
white expanse

beyond the tree line,
we learned

Buddhist holy men
come again as Orca Whales:

the greater their mastery,
the further back in time.

James Bertolino

INSIDE PASSAGE

Twelve thousand years passed by
in the blink of leviathan's eye.
Rivers of Pleistocene ice

still gouge and grind through rock and rime,
leaving in their wake a place where time gone
is not regretted.

Here, pinks pirouette, seemingly happily,
on the way to their conclusion.
They practice

their leap of life, before
they are devoured by the mouths
of rivers and streams that draw them in,

even against the flow. Silvers break,
slice the surface in tandem, ripples rise,
are swallowed, rise again.

If I would look with eyes not dimmed
by dreams or desires, by foolishness or fears,
could I unearth an instant, within a blink,

that's as clean as a breaching breath,
flukes saluting, slapping in unison,
before returning to the sea?

Cynthia Neely

LAMENT OF THE ORCAS

Of course we remember how it began.
We never forget: Seeds of trees
entered earth, swelling into forests.
Rain brought fertile streams.
Water brought salmon.
When everything was ready, we rose up
from the Kingdom of the Dead,
dressed in our very best.
You followed. We were friends then,
sharing the feast of the sea,
but now we have fallen out. You have
trapped us and made us beg for food.
But, as we swim side by side, speaking
our private languages, we tell our story
over and over, so none of us forgets:
First came trees, then streams and fish.
We found our prey through sound.
Now noise chases us through barren tides
into seas of hunger we do not understand.

Sheila Nickerson

SAFE SAILING

If we thought more in terms of pod,
if we swam together, moving left
then right, if we spoke in musical
highs and lows, if we always ate our
meals together, then we would fill
the sea both day and night, our
sleek skinned boats careening
through silky water, sprouting a
loving community, a pod of seeds
that cannot be lost.

Nancy Canyon

ABOUT THE SEADOC SOCIETY

The SeaDoc Society is a flagship program of the Karen C. Drayer Wildlife Health Center, a center of excellence at the world-famous UC Davis School of Veterinary Medicine. As "doctors" of the sea, we use science and education to improve the health of the Salish Sea and its marine wildlife. We are leaders in conducting marine wildlife research and work to ensure that science plays an active role in addressing the most urgent marine health challenges facing the Salish Sea.

One example is the recovery of endangered Southern Resident killer whales. Early on, SeaDoc led the charge to evaluate the health of these unique animals. We assessed the threat infectious diseases could play in their recovery and found that very little was known about orcas' diseases. To address this, we championed a killer whale stranding response protocol to learn why animals stranded and died. We later created an electronic medical records database for this population and participated in the first-ever medical intervention of a sick, free-ranging Southern Resident whale. Also, we helped develop the regional protocol for keeping them out of a slick should an oil spill occur. Currently SeaDoc's Science Director serves on the Governor's Task Force to recover Southern Resident killer whales.

We don't do this work alone. SeaDoc is proud to partner actively with the Center for Whale Research, Fisheries and Oceans Canada, National Marine Mammal Foundation, NOAA Fisheries, SeaWorld, Vancouver Aquarium, Washington State Department of Fish and Wildlife, Whale Museum, Whale Sanctuary Project, and many others.

Joseph K. Gaydos

Wildlife Veterinarian and Science Director, SeaDoc Society

Editors' Note: Proceeds from this anthology benefit the SeaDoc Society.

CONTRIBUTORS

Kelli Russell Agodon's most recent book, *Hourglass Museum*, was a Finalist for the Washington State Book Awards and shortlisted for the Julie Suk Prize in Poetry. Her other books include *The Daily Poet: Day-By-Day Prompts For Your Writing Practice* and *Letters from the Emily Dickinson Room*, Winner of the Foreword Book of the Year Prize for poetry and Washington State Book Award Finalist. Kelli is the cofounder of Two Sylvias Press and Co-Director of Poets on the Coast: A Weekend Writing Retreat for Women in Washington State. agodon.com / twosylviaspress.com

Luther Allen facilitates SpeakEasy, a community reading series, and is co-editor of *Noisy Water*. His collection of poems is *The View from Lummi Island* (Other Mind, 2010). His work is included in the recent anthologies *WA 129*; *Refugium: Poems for the Pacific*; *Poets Unite! LitFUSE @10*; and *Weaving the Terrain*. His short story, *The Stilled Ring*, was finalist in the annual fiction contest at *Terrain.org*.

James Bertolino's poetry has received recognition through a Book-of-the-Month Club Poetry Fellowship, the Discovery Award, a National Endowment for the Arts fellowship, two *Quarterly Review of Literature* book publication awards, and the Jeanne Lohmann Poetry Prize for Washington State Poets. His fourteenth volume of poems is *Ravenous Bliss: New and Selected Love* Poems (MoonPath, 2014). His latest book is the anthology he edited, *Last Call: The Anthology of Beer, Wine & Spirits Poetry* (World Enough Writers, 2018).

Yvonne Blomer served as the city of Victoria's Poet Laureate 2015-2018. Recent books include *Sugar Ride: Cycling from Hanoi to Kuala Lumpur* (Palimpsest, 2017) and *As if a Raven* (Palimpsest, 2014). *Refugium: Poems for the Pacific* (editor, Caitlin, 2017) is the first in a trilogy of water-focused environmental poetry anthologies Yvonne is editing. Yvonne won the Overleaf Chapbook Contest 2017 for *Elegies for Earth*. She lives, works and raises her family on the traditional territories of the WSÁNEĆ (Saanich), Lkwungen (Songhees), Wyomilth (Esquimalt) peoples of the Coast Salish Nation. She gives thanks for the privilege of being there.

Anita K. Boyle is an artist and poet who lives outside Bellingham, WA. Her books include *Bamboo Equals Loon, What the Alder Told Me, and The Drenched.* Her poems can be found in *Bracken; Crab Creek Review; Clover, A Literary Rag;* and other literary magazines. Anita makes paper and books, assemblages, prints, and paintings. To learn more about her art and poetry, visit her website at EgressStudio.com or her blog at egressstudio.wordpress.com.

Allen Braden has published in *The Times Literary Supplement, Virginia Quarterly Review, The New Republic, Orion* and elsewhere. A recipient of fellowships from the NEA and Artist Trust as well as the Dorothy Sargent Rosenberg Prize, Braden is the author of *A Wreath of Down and Drops of Blood* (University of Georgia, 2010) and *Elegy in the Passive Voice* (University of Alaska Fairbanks).

Jennifer Bullis is author of the chapbook *Impossible Lessons* (MoonPath). Her poems and essays appear in *Gulf Coast, Terrain.org, Water~Stone Review, Tinderbox Poetry Journal,* and *Iron Horse.* Her book-length manuscripts have been finalists for the Brittingham & Felix Pollak Poetry Prizes and the Moon City Poetry Award. Originally from Reno, she earned a Ph.D. in English and taught at Whatcom Community College in Bellingham for 14 years. Currently she is librettist for a cantata in the voices of the mythical Sirens, to be performed by Burning River Baroque of Cleveland and Seattle Baroque Orchestra.

Nancy Canyon holds the MFA in Creative Writing from PLU, 2007. She has authored *Struck,* a memoir detailing her work as a fire lookout attendant in the 1970s; *Saltwater,* a book of poetry; *Dark Forest,* an ebook of short-short fiction; and three novels. Her poetry and prose is published in the anthology *Last Call; Nature's Healing Spirit; Ice Cream Poems; Songs of Ourselves; Water~Stone Review; Fourth Genre; Floating Bridge Review;* and *Clover, A Literary Rag,* and other journals. Ms. Canyon can be found writing and/or painting in her Morgan Block artist studio located in historic Fairhaven, a district of Bellingham, WA.

Poet and paper artist **Terry Ann Carter,** is the author of six collections of poetry and five haiku chapbooks. *TOKAIDO* (Red Moon, 2017) won the Touchstone Distinguished Book Award. She is the past president of Haiku Canada and facilitator for the Haiku Arbutus Study Group in Victoria, B.C.

Susan Chase-Foster writes in Raven's Roost, a small cottage in Bellingham, WA, near the edge of the Salish Sea, where salmon, cetaceans and great blue herons have historically hung out. Inspired by seafolk migrations, she frequently writes in lands bordered by the Arctic Ocean, the South China and Tasman Seas, and the Pacific Ocean. Her poems have appeared in *Cirque*, *Clover*, and other Pacific Rim publications. She is the author of *Xièxiè Taipei, Poems and Images from Taiwan*, and *Through Choking Smoke*, a chapbook. Susan is currently penning "poemoirs" of her travels through New Zealand.

Barbara Clarke's memoir, *Getting to Home: Sojourn in a Perfect House*, was published in 2009. "How Many Writing Books Does It Take?" appeared in the 2010 debut issue of *Line Zero*, a literary-arts magazine. Her essay "Good Vibrations," was published in the online magazine *Full Grown People* in 2015. Memoir pieces "Thank You Grace Paley" and "Tis the Season" were published in recent Red Wheelbarrow Writers anthologies. She is currently at work on *The Opposite of Hate: A Memoir*.

Christine Clarke is a scientist and poet whose poetry has appeared in *Clover, A Literary Rag; DMQ Review; Raven Chronicles; Poets Unite: The LitFuse @10 Anthology; Emerald Reflections: A South Seattle Emerald Anthology;* The City of Seattle's Poetry on Buses (where a previous version of "Return to Salish Sea" appeared). She has been nominated twice for a Pushcart Prize. At Lime Kiln State Park, she first encountered Southern resident orcas as she watched three generations of K Pod play in the kelp at her feet. She remains awestruck.

Sarah DeWeerdt is a freelance science writer based in Seattle, and she is grateful to live and work in the ancestral territories of the Duwamish and Coast Salish peoples. Her journalism covering biology, medicine, and the environment has appeared in publications including *Anthropocene, Nautilus, Nature, Newsweek*, and *Spectrum*. Her poetry was part of the 2014 "Secrets of the Sea" exhibit at the University of Southern Maine's Atrium Art Gallery. Find her on Twitter at @DeWeerdt_Sarah

Chelsea Dingman's first book, *Thaw*, was chosen by Allison Joseph to win the National Poetry Series (University of Georgia, 2017). She is also the author of the chapbook, *What Bodies Have I Moved* (Madhouse, 2018). She has won prizes such as: *The Southeast* Review's Gearhart Poetry Prize, The *Sycamore Review's* Wabash Prize, *Water~Stone Review's* Jane Kenyon Poetry Prize, and The South Atlantic Modern Language Association's Creative Writing Award for Poetry. Her work is forthcoming in *Redivider, New England Review,* and *The Southern Review,* among others. Visit her website: chelseadingman.com.

Victoria Doerper writes memoir, poetry, and non-fiction from her home near the shore of the Salish Sea. Her poetry appears in *Noisy Water: Poetry from Whatcom County, Washington; Last Call: The Anthology of Beer, Wine, & Spirits Poetry; Clover, A Literary Rag; Cirque, A Literary Journal for the North Pacific Rim;* and *The Plum Tree Tavern.* Her prose appears in *Orion Magazine.*

Heather Durham is the author of *Going Feral: Field Notes on Wonder and Wanderlust* (Trail to Table, 2019). She holds a Master of Science in Environmental Biology from Antioch New England University and a Master of Fine Arts from the Northwest Institute of Literary Arts. She's held a variety of environmental jobs around the country from interpretive park ranger to field biologist, trails worker to restoration ecologist. She currently lives in the foothills of the Washington Cascades where she works at Wilderness Awareness School.

Ryler Dustin's poems appear or are forthcoming in *The Best of Iron Horse, American Life in Poetry, Gulf Coast, The Best of Button Poetry,* and elsewhere. He holds an MFA from the University of Houston and a Ph.D. from the University of Nebraska—Lincoln. A native of Bellingham, he has represented Seattle on the final stage of the Individual World Poetry Slam. His book, *Heavy Lead Birdsong,* is available from Write Bloody Publishing. You can reach him through rylerdustin.com.

Once a wildlife biologist, **Seren Fargo** now incorporates her love of the natural world in her poetry. In 2009, she began writing haiku and established the Bellingham Haiku Group, which she currently co-coordinates. Her work has expanded to include other types of Japanese short-form poetry, such as tanka and collaborative haiku. She has also recently begun experimenting with haiga. Her work has won awards and has been published internationally. She resides on a beautiful wooded lot she shares with several chipmunks, red squirrels, juncos, jays, and barred owls.

Daryl Farmer is the author of *Where We Land*, a collection of short fiction, and the nonfiction book *Bicycling Beyond the Divide*, which received a Barnes and Noble Discover Award and was a Colorado Book Award finalist. Recent work has been published in such journals as *Hotel Amerika, Talking River,* and *Whitefish Review.* He is currently an Associate Professor at the University of Alaska-Fairbanks where he directs the MFA program and is on faculty at the University of Alaska Anchorage low-residency MFA Program. darylfarmer.com. Instagram.com/big_strong_boy.

Gail Folkins often writes about her deep roots in the American West. She is the author of a memoir titled *Light in the Trees,* named a 2016 Foreword INDIES finalist in the nature category, and *Texas Dance Halls: A Two-Step Circuit.* Folkins teaches creative writing at Hugo House in Seattle. Her website is gailfolkins.com. Follow her @gailfolkins.

Bob Friel is an award-winning writer, photographer and filmmaker who lives on Orcas Island. He is the author of three books: *Underwater Maldives* and *Underwater Bahamas* include collections of his marine photos; *The Barefoot Bandit: The True Tale of Colton Harris-Moore, New American Outlaw* is a true crime bestseller. Friel also produces the science/adventure video series *Salish Sea Wild!* for the SeaDoc Society (salishseawild.org), and is a volunteer with the Large Whale Entanglement Response Network and the Marine Mammal Stranding Network. bobfriel.com.

Yvonne Garrett's degrees include MFA in Fiction (The New School), an MA-Irish Studies (NYU), MLIS-Archives (Palmer), MA-Humanities (NYU), and she is working on a Ph.D. (Drew University). Senior Fiction Editor at Black Lawrence Press, she also edits the publishing newsletter *Sapling.* Her writing has appeared in *The Baltimore Review, The Brooklyn Rail, Publishers Weekly, Alternative Press,* and *Thrash Metal* among others. Her sixth poetry chapbook with ME Sanger is *split open the sky: eternity overwhelms me* (Aoxlotl River). She's taught creative writing at Manhattanville College and the Brooklyn Veteran's Center. www.yvonnegarrett.com @yvonnePRB

Joseph K. (Joe) Gaydos is a Senior Wildlife Veterinarian and is the Science Director for the SeaDoc Society. For almost two decades, Joe has been working on wildlife and ecosystem health issues in the Pacific

Northwest and has authored several books on the Salish Sea. He studies killer whale health and currently serves on the Governor's Task Force for Southern Resident killer whale recovery. Joe's a science nerd with a passion for all things wild: wildlife, wild places and wild people.

Jessica Gigot is a poet, farmer, teacher and musician. She has a small farm in Bow, WA called Harmony Fields that makes artisan sheep cheese and grows organic herbs. Her first book of poems, *Flood Patterns*, was published by Antrim House Books in 2015 and her writing has been published in several regional and national journals, including *Orion*, *Floating Bridge Press Review*, *Pilgrimage*, *About Place Journal*, and *Poetry Northwest*. Her writing website is www.jessicagigot.com but the farm one works too www.harmonyfields.com. Her Instagram and Twitter handle is: @shepherdessjess.

Mary Elizabeth Gillilan lives a little south of Mt. Temporary. Good family. Good friends. Best dog ever. She practices gratitude. The first time she saw a whale was in Prince William Sound on a fishing boat. She thought it was an island. She is the editor of *Clover, a Literary Rag*. Gives thanks to everyone who awarded *Clover* with a Bellingham, Washington Mayor's Arts Award in 2017. Sometimes crazy works out. independentwritersstudio.com.

Iris Graville is the author of three nonfiction books: *Hands at Work, BOUNTY,* and a memoir, *Hiking Naked*. She lives on Lopez Island, WA where she publishes *SHARK REEF Literary Magazine* and contributes regularly to *The Wayfarer Magazine*. Sometimes you'll find her on the interisland ferry, working on a new essay collection about the Salish Sea, climate change, and Washington State Ferries. irisgraville.com.

Carol Guess is the author of twenty books of poetry and prose. She teaches in the MFA Creative Writing program at Western Washington University. Follow her here: carolguess.blogspot.com.

Sam Hamill was Founding Editor of Copper Canyon Press and served as editor there 32 years. His 40+ published books include 17 volumes of original poetry, four collections of literary essays, and celebrated translations. For thirty years, Hamill was associated with the Port Townsend Writers Conference, including ten years as director. In 2003, declining an invitation to the White House, he founded Poets Against the

War, collecting 30,000 poems by 26,000 poets, the largest anthology in recorded history. His collected poems, *Habitation*, was published by Lost Horse Press in 2014. He died in 2018 at his home in Anacortes, Washington.

Alaska Writer Laureate 2016-2018, **Ernestine Saankaláxt Hayes** is the author of American Book Award recipient *Blonde Indian, an Alaska Native Memoir*, which also received an Honoring Alaska Indigenous Literature Award and was finalist for the Kiriyama Prize and PEN Nonfiction Award. Grandmother of four and great-grandmother of three, Hayes is a professor at the University of Alaska Southeast. Her latest book, *The Tao of Raven*, places fiction and nonfiction narratives in the context of Raven and the Box of Daylight and Sun Tzu's *Art of War*. Hayes belongs to the Wolf House of the Kaagwaantaan clan of the Tlingit nation.

Christopher Howell has published eleven collections of poems, most recently *Love's Last Number* (Milkweed Editions, 2017). A new collection will be forthcoming from the University of Washington Press in 2019. Other recent work may be found in the pages of *Field, Poetry International, Gettysburg Review* and *Miramar*. He taught at universities in Massachusetts, Colorado, Oregon and Kansas before becoming part of the MFA faculty at Eastern Washington University, where he is director of Willow Springs Books. He has also been, for many years, director and principal editor for Lynx House Press.

Holly J. Hughes is the author or editor of six books, most recently the chapbook *Passings,* which received an American Book Award in 2017. A graduate of Pacific Lutheran's MFA program, she's served on the staff for the last decade. She's grateful to have spent time among orcas during thirty summers working on the water in Alaska on boats ranging from kayaks to cruise ships, including skippering a 65-foot schooner. She currently leads writing and mindfulness workshops and consults as a writing coach, dividing her time between the Chimacum valley and a log cabin built in Indianola, Washington. hollyjhughes.com

Julie B. Hunter has written poems and stories about and with children for the past 33 years as a public school teacher. Currently the library media specialist at Wade King Elementary in Bellingham, Julie explores and enjoys literature with students daily. She and her husband Mark raised their two sons on Lummi Island, spending countless hours on the west shore, always hopeful for an orca visitation. A long-time member of Congregation Beth Israel, Julie was moved to express her grief over Tahlequah's loss as a poem during a break in services on Yom Kippur.

Devin Kelly is the author of *In This Quiet Church of Night, I Say Amen* (Civil Coping Mechanisms), and the winner of a Best of the Net Prize. He lives and teaches high school in New York City.

Nima Kian is an Iranian-American poet. As part of the Iranian diaspora, his writing investigates the divide between time—the space that is time—and time—the clock that serves as time's arbitrator. A perpetual immigrant, he experienced three continents of life and continues to explore the Iranian experience, following the movement of a people across time. His poems aim to discover the moments in (his) history when particular changes impacted a people's trajectory. He teaches writing in the East Bay Area.

A Pushcart and Best of the Net nominee, **J.I. Kleinberg** is co-editor of *56 Days of August* (Five Oaks Press 2017), and *Noisy Water: Poetry from Whatcom County, Washington* (Other Mind Press 2015), and co-produces the Bellingham-based SpeakEasy poetry series. Her poetry has appeared in *One, Diagram, WA129, Otoliths, Raven Chronicles, Calamus Journal*, and elsewhere. She lives in Bellingham, WA, and blogs at chocolateisaverb.wordpress.com and poetrydepartmentwordpress.com.

Jenne Knight writes poetry and essays, and her work appears in *The Rumpus, Bodega, Barnstorm*, and *The Common*, among others. Her poem, "Elegy for My Father," was nominated for Best of the Net 2016. For more information, please visit jenneknight.com.

Jenifer Browne Lawrence is the author of *Grayling* (Perugia, 2015), and *One Hundred Steps from Shore* (Blue Begonia, 2006). Awards include the Perugia Press Prize, the Orlando Poetry Prize, the James Hearst Poetry Prize, the Potomac Review Poetry Award, and a GAP grant from Artist Trust. She has been a resident at Hedgebrook, Soapstone, Willapa Bay AIR, and Centrum. Her work appears in *Bracken, The Coachella Review, Los Angeles Review, Narrative, North American Review*, and elsewhere. Jenifer lives on Puget Sound, and edits the Seattle-based journal, *Crab Creek Review*. Come say hello on Twitter @jeniferbrowne or Instagram @lawrence.jenifer.

David M. Laws is pretty confused about life, but works hard to make sense of small pieces of the world. He reads, walks his dog, plays gin rummy with his wonderful wife of 37 years, gardens, writes poetry and music, plays several different sizes of saxophone and flute as well as piano, repairs musical instruments, and dreams of a model railroad empire to rule with an iron hand. He has lived in Bellingham for 25 years and will not willingly leave, so please don't ask.

Mark Leiren-Young wrote and directed the award-winning documentary, *The Hundred-Year-Old Whale*—the story of Granny. He's currently in post-production on a documentary adaptation of his award-winning book about Moby Doll—*The Killer Whale Who Changed the World*. He hosts the popular podcast, *Skaana*, about orcas, oceans and the environment. His latest book *Orcas Everywhere*—a science book for young readers—is being released by Orca Book Publishers in the fall of 2019. leiren-young.com @leirenyoung Follow Mark's "pod" cast at skaana.org

Rob Lewis is a poet, writer and house painter, whose main work is bringing the power of language to the defense of the more-than-human world. His writings have been published in *Dark Mountain, Cascadia Weekly, Manzanita, The Atlanta Review, The Southern Review* and others. As owner of Earth Craft Painting, he also works to revive the use of local wild clays to paint our work and living spaces.

Priscilla Long writes poetry, creative nonfiction, fiction, science, and history. She has authored six books, including *The Writer's Portable Mentor*, second edition (University of New Mexico), and a collection of personal essays, *Fire and Stone: Where Do We Come From? What Are We? Where Are We Going?* (University of Georgia). Her book of poems is *Crossing Over* (University of New Mexico). She is also author of *Minding the Muse: A Handbook for Composers, Painters, Writers, and Other Creators.* Her history of coal mining is *Where the Sun Never Shines: A History of America's Bloody Coal Industry.* priscillalong.com.

Paula MacKay is a freelance writer/researcher, field biologist, and communications consultant for conservation. For the past two decades, she has studied terrestrial carnivores with her husband, Dr. Robert Long (Woodland Park Zoo), with whom she currently monitors wolverines in the North

Cascades. Paula served as managing editor for *Noninvasive Survey Methods for Carnivores* (Island, 2008) and earned an MFA in creative writing from Pacific Lutheran University in 2015. She has written for numerous nonprofits, books, scientific journals, and magazines. Some of her recent work can be seen in *Wild Hope, Earth Island Journal, Inside Ecology,* and *American Forests.*

Carole MacRury resides in Point Roberts, Washington, a unique peninsula and border town that inspires her work. Her poems have won awards and been published worldwide, and her photographs have been featured on the covers of numerous poetry journals and anthologies. She is the author of *In the Company of Crows: Haiku and Tanka Between the Tides* (Black Cat, 2008, 2nd Printing, 2018) and *The Tang of Nasturtiums,* an award-winning e-chapbook (Snapshot 2012).

David Mason was born in Bellingham, Washington, and grew up sailing, fishing, biking and playing throughout the Puget Sound region, as well as in Alaska. He served as Colorado poet laureate from 2010 to 2014, and teaches at The Colorado College. His many books include *Ludlow: A Verse Novel; Voices, Places: Essays; Sea Salt: Poems of a Decade; Davey McGravy: Tales to be Read Aloud to Children and Adult Children;* and *The Sound: New and Selected Poems.* Currently he divides his time between Colorado and Tasmania.

Christen Mattix is the author of *Skein: The Heartbreaks and Triumphs of a Long Distance Knitter,* experimental notebook journalism about loneliness and connection in a fast-paced world. She is founder and poetry editor of The Poem Booth Project, a former phone booth displaying poems by local poets (poembooth.weebly.com). She's taught at Western Washington University and The Jansen Art Center. Her essays and poetry have been published in The Meeting House, Shoreline City Art Zine, *Psaltery & Lyre,* and *Clover, A Literary Rag.* Mattix grew up in Thailand and moved to Bellingham, WA where she continues to make a ruckus. christenmattix.com.

Tim McNulty is a poet, essayist, and nature writer. His most recent poetry collection, *Ascendance,* was published by Pleasure Boat Studio. Earlier poetry collections include *In Blue Mountain Dusk,* and *Pawtracks.* His *Olympic National Park, A Natural History* was reissued in a new edition in 2018. McNulty's poems, essays, criticism, and articles have appeared in numerous publications, and his natural history writings have been translated into German, Chinese, and Japanese. He has received the Washington State

Book Award and National Outdoor Book Award, among other honors. He lives in the foothills of the Olympic Mountains. Tim's website is timmcnultypoet.com.

Brenda Miller is the author of five essay collections, most recently *An Earlier Life* (Ovenbird Books, 2016). She also co-authored *Tell It Slant: Creating, Refining and Publishing Creative Nonfiction* and *The Pen and The Bell: Mindful Writing in a Busy World.* Her poetry has appeared or is forthcoming in *Tupelo Quarterly, Sweet, Bellevue Literary Review, and Psaltery & Lyre.* Her work has received six Pushcart Prizes. She is a Professor of English at Western Washington University, and associate faculty at the Rainier Writing Workshop. Her website is brendamillerwriter.com.

JM Miller is a trans-identified poet, essayist, instructor and healer living on a 10-acre organic farm on Vashon Island, WA. They won the Grand Prize for the Eco Arts Awards in 2014 and were a finalist for *Terrain.org*'s 2013 poetry contest. Miller teaches poetry and creative nonfiction writing at the University of Washington in Tacoma and is an instructor at Richard Hugo House. JM's chapbook, Primitive Elegy, was published by alice blue books, and their work can be found at *Poecology, Bellingham Review, Cimarron Review, Columbia Poetry Review, CURA, Whitefish Review* and others.

Jim Milstead retired from the Multiversity of Uniformia at Berkeley, California, after many years of rearing insects for biological control research projects. While in Bellingham he was a member of IWS, the Village Books Poetry Group, and the Personal Writing, Memoir, Play, Brainstorm, and Taking Charge groups at the Senior Center. Called *The Bard of Bellingham*, Jim recently claimed himself *DisBard* and moved to the Bay Area where so much of his story began. Following the success of his first book of poetry, *Collage*, he has just authored a second called *Scenario*, and is at work on a third.

Jed Myers lives in Seattle. He is author of *Watching the Perseids* (Sacramento Poetry Center Book Award), *The Marriage of Space and Time* (MoonPath, 2019), and three chapbooks, including *Dark's Channels* (Iron Horse Literary Review Chapbook Award). Recent recognitions include the Prime Number Magazine Award for Poetry, *The Southeast Review*'s Gearhart Poetry Prize, and *The Tishman Review*'s Edna St. Vincent Millay Poetry Prize. Recent poems can be found in *Rattle, Poetry Northwest, The American Journal of Poetry,*

Southern Poetry Review, The Greensboro Review, Terrain.org, Valparaiso Poetry Review, Solstice, and elsewhere. He is Poetry Editor for the journal *Bracken.* jedmyers.com.

JS Nahani's poetry and prose have appeared in *Poem Booth Bellingham, VoiceCatcher, The Haro, I Want You To Know, Three Minus One,* and *Berkeley Arts Gallery.* She holds a Masters in Social Work with continuing education in Expressive Arts and Dance Movement Therapy. Through her business and practice of Creative Insights (creativeinsightswithjay.com), Nahani works 1:1 and with groups, helping people to connect to their truths and transform through expression. She lives with her family, next door to a horse and a donkey, in Bellingham, Washington.

Cynthia Neely is the author of three chapbooks, including winner of the *Flyway: Journal of Writing and Environment* Hazel Lipa Prize for *Broken Water,* and the *Bright Hill Press* chapbook prize for *Passing Through Blue Earth.* Her full-length collection, *Flight Path,* was a finalist in the *Aldrich Press* book contest. Her poetry appears in many journals including, *Bellevue Literary Review, Crab Creek Review* and *Terrain.org.* Her essays appear in *The Writers' Chronicle* and *Cutthroat Journal* (runner up for the Barry Lopez prize in Creative Non-fiction) and *Terrain.org.*

Paul E. Nelson founded SPLAB (Seattle Poetics LAB) & the Cascadia Poetry Festival. Since 1993, SPLAB's produced hundreds of poetry events, 600 hours of interviews with Allen Ginsberg, Michael McClure, Joanne Kyger, Nate Mackey and Brenda Hillman, among others. Published books include *American Sentences* (2015), *A Time Before Slaughter* (2010), *Organic in Cascadia: A Sequence of Energies* (2013) and his 2015 interview with Cuban poet José Kozer was published as *Tiovivo Tres Amigos* (2016). Co-Editor of *Make It True: Poetry From Cascadia* and *56 Days of August: Poetry Postcards,* Paul is engaged in a 20-year bioregional cultural investigation of Cascadia, and serves as literary executor for the late poet Sam Hamill.

Sheila Nickerson, a former Poet Laureate of Alaska, lives in Bellingham, WA. Her most recent book of poetry is *Hitchhiking the Highway of Tears* (MoonPath, 2017). Her most recent prose work is *Blackbird Flying: A Memoir* (Fuze Publishing, January 2019). Other works include *Disappearance: A Map; Midnight to the North;* and *Harnessed to the Pole: Sledge Dogs in Service to American Explorers of the Arctic, 1853-1909.*

J.L. Oakley writes award-winning historical fiction spanning the 19th century to WWII, with characters who stand up for something in their own time and place. Her books have been recognized with a 2013 Bellingham Mayor's Arts Award, the 2013 Chanticleer Grand Prize for *Tree Soldier*, and the 2016 Goethe Award Grand Prize for *The Jøssing Affair*, among others. Her latest novel, *Mist-Chi-Mas*, is a 2018 WILLA Award finalist and a 2018 Will Rogers Silver Medallion Award winner. She lives in Bellingham, WA, loves Northwest history, and writes every day.

Rebecca Hart Olander's poetry has appeared recently in *Ilanot Review, Mom Egg Review, Plath Poetry Project, Radar Poetry, Solstice,* and *Yemassee Journal,* among others. Collaborative work made with Elizabeth Paul has been published in *They Said: A Multi-Genre Anthology of Contemporary Collaborative Writing* (BLP) and online at *Duende* and *petrichor.* Rebecca won the 2013 Women's National Book Association poetry contest, and her first chapbook will be out with dancing girl press in the fall of 2019. She lives in Western Massachusetts, where she teaches writing at Westfield State University and is the editor/director of Perugia Press.
Social media: @rholanderpoet. rebeccahartolander.com.

Nancy Pagh was born in Anacortes, WA and burst on to the literary scene as a teenager, publishing "Is a Clam Clammy, Or Is It Just Wet?" in a local boating magazine. Since then she has authored three collections of (more serious) poetry and her work appears in many anthologies and periodicals. She is the author of *Write Moves: A Creative Writing Guide & Anthology* and *At Home Afloat: Women on the Waters of the Pacific Northwest.* She teaches at Western Washington University in Bellingham, where she won the 2018 Kleinknecht Award for Teaching Excellence. More at nancypagh.com.

Dayna Patterson is the author of *If Mother Braids a Waterfall,* from Signature Books (2020). Her creative work has appeared recently in *AGNI, Hotel Amerika, So to Speak, Sugar House Review, Western Humanities Review,* and *Zone 3.* She is a former managing editor of *Bellingham Review,* founding editor-in-chief of *Psaltery & Lyre,* and poetry editor for *Exponent II Magazine.* She is a co-editor of *Dove Song: Heavenly Mother in Mormon Poetry* (Peculiar Pages, 2018). daynapatterson.com.

Craig Santos Perez is a native Chamorro from the Pacific Island of Guam. He is the author of four collections of poetry and the co-editor of three anthologies of Pacific literature. He teaches eco-poetry at the University of Hawaiʻi, Mānoa.

Poet and photographer **Ronda Piszk Broatch** is the author of *Lake of Fallen Constellations*, (MoonPath, 2015). Seven-time Pushcart Prize nominee, Ronda is the recipient of an Artist Trust GAP Grant, a May Swenson Poetry Award finalist, and former editor of *Crab Creek Review*. Her journal publications include *Atlanta Review, Blackbird, Prairie Schooner, Fourteen Hills, Mid-American Review*, Public Radio KUOW's *All Things Considered*, and *Sycamore Review*.

Rena Priest's debut collection, *Patriarchy Blues*, was released by MoonPath Press, and garnered an American Book Award. Her chapbook, *Sublime Subliminal*, was released on Floating Bridge Press in 2018. She was selected by Kathleen Flenniken as a 2019 Jack Straw Writer. With support from the National Geographic Explorer program, she is presently writing about regional efforts to repatriate an orca from an amusement park in Florida. Her work can be found in *Diagram, Sweet Tree Review, Cosmonauts Avenue*, and elsewhere. She is a Lummi Tribal member and holds an MFA in Writing from Sarah Lawrence College. Learn more at renapriest.com.

Diane Raptosh's fourth poetry collection, *American Amnesiac* (Etruscan) was longlisted for the 2013 National Book Award. The recipient of the Idaho Governor's Arts Award in Excellence (2018), she is a three-time State of Idaho Literature Fellow. She has served as Boise Poet Laureate (2013) amd Idaho Writer-in-Residence (2013-2016). She has given poetry workshops everywhere from riverbanks to maximum-security prisons. She teaches creative writing and runs the program in Criminal Justice/Prison Studies at The College of Idaho. Her sixth book of poems, *Dear Z: The Zygote Epistles*, will be published by Etruscan Press in 2020. dianeraptosh.com. FB: DianeJRaptosh Twitter: @DianeRaptosh

Bethany Reid's latest book of poems is *Body My House* (2018). Her book, *Sparrow*, won the 2012 Gell Poetry Prize. Her work has recently appeared in *The Seattle Review, Cheat River Review, Escape into Life (EIL), Willow Springs, Clementine, CALYX*, and the anthology, *All We Can Hold*. In addition to 25 years of teaching college writers, Bethany has taught craft workshops for the It's About Time Writers series, and Write on the Sound. She blogs about writing and life at bethanyareid.com.

Paisley Rekdal is the author of six books of poetry, most recently *Nightengale* (Copper Canyon, 2019). A former Guggenheim and NEA fellow, she is the current poet laureate of Utah.

Rachel Rose is the author of four collections of poetry, including *Marry & Burn*, and a memoir, *The Dog Lover Unit: Lessons in Courage from the World's K9 Cops*, (St. Martin's), which was shortlisted for the 2018 Arthur Ellis award for best non-fiction crime book. She received a Pushcart Prize in 2014 and 2016. A former fellow at The University of Iowa's International Writing Program, she is the Poet Laureate Emerita of Vancouver. rachelsprose.weebly.com

Adrienne Ross Scanlan is the author of *Turning Homeward: Restoring Hope and Nature in the Urban Wild* (Washington State Book Award 2017 Finalist). Her work has appeared in *City Creatures Blog*, *LabLit: The Culture of Science in Fiction & Fact*, and other publications. She received an Artist Trust Literature Fellowship, was the nonfiction editor for the *Blue Lyra Review*, and is a reviewer for the *New York Journal of Books*. Adrienne has a Certificate in Editing from the University of Washington and is a freelance developmental editor. You can reach her at adrienne-ross-scanlan.com / adrienne@adrienne-ross-scanlan.com.

Stan Sanvel Rubin's work has appeared in such magazines as *The Georgia Review*, *Iowa Review*, *Poetry Northwest*, *Ascent*, *Florida Review*, *Shanghai Poetry Review* and *Agni*. His fourth full collection, *There. Here.* was published by Lost Horse Press in 2013. His third, *Hidden Sequel*, won the Barrow Street Poetry Book Prize. He lives on the northern Olympic Peninsula of Washington State. stansanvelrubin.com @cosmicmemory

Essayist, poet, and marine biologist **Eva Saulitis** for nearly thirty years studied killer whales in Prince William Sound, along with her partner Craig Matkin. Her poems are collected in two books: *Many Ways to Say It* and *Prayer in Wind*. Her memoir *Into Great Silence: A Memoir of Discovery and Loss among Vanishing Orcas* charts time with orcas during and after the Exxon Valdez oil spill, and her essay collection, *Leaving Resurrection: Chronicles of a Whale Scientist*, recounts her experiences as a marine biologist in Alaska. Eva wrote *Becoming Earth* when she knew that her health would not return. She was a much-beloved teacher, mentor, and friend.

Tina Schumann is a Pushcart-nominated poet and author of three poetry collections, *As If* (Parlor City, 2010) which was awarded the Stephen Dunn Poetry Prize, *Requiem: A Patrimony of Fugues* (Diode Editions, 2016) winner of the Diode Editions 2016 Chapbook contest, and *Praising the Paradox* (Red Hen, 2019.) She is editor of the award-winning anthology *Two-Countries: U.S. Daughters & Sons of Immigrant Parents* (Red Hen, 2017). Her poems have seen publication since 1999 including *The American Journal of Poetry, Ascent, Cimarron Review, Michigan Quarterly Review, Nimrod, Parabola, Palabra* and *Verse Daily*. Read more at tinaschumann.com.

Betty Scott is an award-winning poet whose poems have appeared in *WA 129; Clover; Noisy Water; Cirque Journal; Floating Bridge Press* and other publications and anthologies in Canada and the Northwest. In 2018 *Central Heating: Poems that Celebrate Love, Loss and Planet Earth* was published by Cave Moon Press of Yakima, WA. Scott is often accompanied by J.P. Falcon Grady who writes, "I am a proud member of the Piikani (Blackfeet) tribe, a self-taught singer / songwriter / guitarist who intertwines acoustic melodies and vocals, finding inspiration in Betty's words." Scott is currently writing a collection of short stories. Her website is bettyscottwriter.com.

Carla Shafer's poems appear in *Whatcom Places II; Peace Poems,* an anthology of international poets. A Sue C. Boynton poetry winner, her recent chapbook is *Remembering the Path.* She founded Bellingham's first open mic, Chuckanut Sandstone Writers Theater in 1991. She is honored as a Writers International Network Poetry Ambassador.

Derek Sheffield's book of poems, *Through the Second Skin,* was a finalist for the Washington State Book Award. His poems have also appeared in *Poetry, The Georgia Review, The Gettysburg Review, Orion,* and *The Southern Review.* His awards include the James Hearst Poetry Prize and the Sparrow Prize in Poetry. He has received fellowships from Artist Trust and the Sustainable Arts Foundation. He lives with his family in the eastern foothills of the Cascades near Leavenworth, Washington, and is the poetry editor of *Terrain.org.*

Tara K. Shepersky is a taxonomist, poet, essayist, and photographer. Her work is a series of conversations with landscape, exploring how our inner and outer, individual and collective experiences listen, speak, and shape themselves to the land we live beside. Recent essays, poems, photos, and

reviews have appeared in *Shark Reef, Empty Mirror, Cascadia Rising Review,* and *Sky Island Journal,* among others. Tara makes her present home in Oregon's Willamette Valley, with her husband and her primary literary credential, a tuxedo cat called d'Artagnan. Her roots are joyfully tangled up in half a dozen soils of America's west.
Website: pdxpersky.com, Twitter: @pdxpersky, Instagram: @tkspdx

Tim Sherry, a longtime public high school teacher and principal, lives in Tacoma, Washington. With a B.A. in English from Pacific Lutheran University and an M.A. in English from the University of Chicago, he did not publish until 2008. Since then he has had poems published in *Rattle, Crab Creek Review, The Raven Chronicles,* and *Floating Bridge Review* among others. He has been a Pushcart nominee, had his poetry included in anthologies and recognized in contests, and in 2010 was an Artsmith Artist Resident on Orcas Island. His poetry collections include *One of Seven Billion* from Moonpath Press and *Holy Ghost Town* from Cirque Press.

Peggy Shumaker was honored by the Rasmuson Foundation as its Distinguished Artist, and by Artsmith as its Artist of the Year. She served as Alaska State Writer Laureate and received a poetry fellowship from the NEA. Professor emerita from University of Alaska Fairbanks, she teaches in the Rainier Writing Workshop MFA at PLU. Her most recent book is *Cairn,* new and selected poetry and prose. She edits the Boreal Books series and the Alaska Literary Series.

Martha Silano is the author of five poetry books, including *Gravity Assist* (2019), *Reckless Lovely* (2014), and *The Little Office of the Immaculate Conception* (2011), all from Saturnalia Books. She co-authored, with Kelli Russell Agodon, *The Daily Poet: Day-By-Day Prompts For Your Writing Practice.* Martha's poems have appeared in *Paris Review, Poetry,* and *New England Review,* among others. Honors include *North American Review*'s James Hearst Poetry Prize and the *Cincinnati Review*'s Robert and Adele Schiff Award in Poetry. Martha teaches at Bellevue College, near her home in Seattle, WA. @marthasliano. Her website is: marthasilano.net.

Sheila Sondik, poet and printmaker, lives in Bellingham, Washington. Her poetry has appeared in *CALYX, Kettle Blue Review, The Literateur, Raven Chronicles, Floating Bridge Review,* and elsewhere. Egress Studio Press published her chapbook, *Fishing a Familiar Pond: Found Poetry from The*

Yearling, in 2013. She has studied a wide range of Japanese and Chinese art forms and her haiku, tanka, and related verse are in numerous print and online journals. Her website is: sheilasondik.com.

Ana Maria Spagna is author of several books of creative nonfiction including *Reclaimers*, stories of people reclaiming sacred land and water, *Test Ride on the Sunnyland Bus*, winner of the *River Teeth* literary nonfiction prize, and three essay collections, *Potluck*, *Now Go Home*, and *Uplake*, plus a novel for young people, *The Luckiest Scar on Earth*. Her work has been recognized by the Society for Environmental Journalists, the Nautilus Book Awards, and as a three-time finalist for the Washington State Book Award. Her writing appears regularly in journals and magazines including *Orion*, *Ecotone*, *Creative Nonfiction*, *Brevity*, and *High Country News*.

Kim Stafford, founding director of the Northwest Writing Institute at Lewis & Clark College, is the author of a dozen books of poetry and prose, including *The Muses Among Us: Eloquent Listening and Other Pleasures of the Writer's Craft* and *100 Tricks Every Boy Can Do: How My Brother Disappeared*. He has taught writing in dozens of schools and community centers, and in Scotland, Italy, and Bhutan. In May 2018 he was named Oregon's 9th Poet Laureate by Governor Kate Brown. kim-stafford.com.

Joannie Stangeland is the author of the poetry collections *The Scene You See*, *In Both Hands*, and *Into the Rumored Spring*, and three chapbooks. She has been a Pushcart nominee, and her poems have also appeared in *Boulevard*, *Prairie Schooner*, *The Southern Review*, and other journals. She is a student in the Rainier Writing Workshop MFA program. Joannie grew up in Seattle and remembers seeing Namu the "killer whale" in a pen in Elliott Bay when she was six. She also remembers her mother's explanation when Namu drowned trying to escape—that he was lonely.

Scott T. Starbuck's *Hawk on Wire: Ecopoems* was a July 2017 "Editor's Pick" (along with *The Collected Stories of Ray Bradbury*) at Newpages.com, and was selected from over 1,500 books as a 2018 Montaigne Medal Finalist at Eric Hoffer Awards for "the most thought-provoking books." His next book of climate change poems *Carbonfish Blues* features art by Guy Denning whose works of activism, refugees, human vulnerability, and realism are known throughout Europe. Starbuck's climateblog *Trees, Fish, and Dreams* has 42,000 views from about 40 countries, and his "Manifesto from Poet on a Dying Planet" is online at *Split Rock Review*.

Alina Stefanescu was born in Romania and lives in Alabama with four incredible mammals. Find her poems and prose in recent issues of *Juked, DIAGRAM, New South, Mantis, VOLT, Cloudbank, New Orleans Review Online,* and others. Her debut fiction collection, *Every Mask I Tried On,* won the Brighthorse Books Prize. She serves as Poetry Editor for *Pidgeonholes* and President of the Alabama State Poetry Society. More arcana online at alinastefanescuwriter.com or @aliner.

M. Stone is a bookworm, birdwatcher, and stargazer living in the foothills of the Blue Ridge Mountains. Her poetry has appeared in *San Pedro River Review, UCity Review,* and numerous other journals. Find her on Twitter @writermstone and at writermstone.wordpress.com.

Ira Sukrungruang is the author of three nonfiction books *Buddha's Dog & other mediations, Southside Buddhist* and *Talk Thai: The Adventures of Buddhist Boy;* the short story collection *The Melting Season;* and the poetry collection *In Thailand It Is Night.* He is president of *Sweet: A Literary Confection* (sweetlit.com), and teaches in the MFA program at University of South Florida. For more information about him, please visit: buddhistboy.com.

Robert Sund (1929-2001) was poet, painter, and calligrapher of the Skagit Valley, and a celebrated presence on the Northwest literary scene. His books include *Poems from Ish River Country: Collected Poems and Translations* (Shoemaker & Hoard), *Taos Mountain* (Poets House), and *Notes from Disappearing Lake* (Pleasure Boat Studio). From his earliest poems, Sund was a strong poetic voice for this region, a place he called the Ish River Country. "Ish" is from the Salish suffix to our river names: Duwamish, Snohomish, Stillaguamish, Samish, Skokomish, Skykomish. It translates roughly as "people of the river." To learn more, visit robertsundpoetshouse.org.

Julie Trimingham has made films, and currently writes essays and fiction. The work closest to her heart concerns the sanctity of the Salish Sea. She lives on an island in traditional Lummi territory.

Jeremy Voigt's poems have appeared in *Gulf Coast, Post Road, Willow Springs, Fifth Wednesday Journal, BPJ,* and other magazines. His chapbook, *Neither Rising nor Falling,* was featured on The Writer's Almanac. He was nominated for a Pushcart Prize by judge Robert Wrigley, and his manuscript, *Estuary,* has been a semi-finalist for the Dorset Prize, The Crab Orchard first book prize, and the Miller Williams prize. He writes, reads, parents, runs, and lives by a large lake in western Washington. jeremyvoigt.com.

Michael Dylan Welch served two terms as poet laureate of Redmond, Washington, where he also curates two poetry reading series. His poems have been performed for the Empress of Japan and at the Baseball Hall of Fame, printed on balloons, and chiseled in stone in New Zealand. In 2012, a translation from the Japanese from one of his books appeared on the back of 150 million U.S. postage stamps. Michael's poetry, essays, reviews, and translations have appeared in hundreds of journals and anthologies. He also runs National Haiku Writing Month (nahaiwrimo.com) and a personal website devoted mostly to poetry (graceguts.com).

Ellen Welcker is the author of *Ram Hands* (Scablands Books, 2016), *The Botanical Garden* (2009 Astrophil Poetry Prize, Astrophil, 2010) and several chapbooks, including "The Pink Tablet" (Fact-Simile Editions, 2018). She lives in Spokane, WA. ellenwelcker.com

Brooke Williams' life has been one of adventure and wilderness exploration. His conservation career spans forty years. His is most recent book, *Open Midnight,* documents his exploration of places where the outer and inner wilderness meet. He's now writing about dragonflies and hermits. He believes that the length of the past equals the length of the future.

Carolyne Wright's most recent book is *This Dream the World: New & Selected Poems* (Lost Horse, 2017), whose title poem received a Pushcart Prize and appeared in *The Best American Poetry 2009.* Her co-edited anthology, *Raising Lilly Ledbetter: Women Poets Occupy the Workspace* (Lost Horse, 2015), received ten Pushcart Prize nominations. A Contributing Editor for the Pushcart Prizes and a Senior Editor for Lost Horse Press, Wright teaches for Richard Hugo House in her native Seattle. She has received fellowships from the NEA, Fulbright Foundation, 4Culture, Seattle's Office of Arts & Culture, and the Instituto Sacatar in Bahia, Brazil. carolynewright.wordpress.com

Maya Jewell Zeller is the author of the interdisciplinary collaboration (with visual artist Carrie DeBacker) *Alchemy For Cells & Other Beasts* (Entre Rios Books, 2017), the chapbook *Yesterday, the Bees* (Floating Bridge, 2015), and the poetry collection *Rust Fish* (Lost Horse, 2011). Recipient of a Promise Award from the Sustainable Arts Foundation as well as a Residency in the H.J. Andrews Experimental Forest, Maya teaches for Central Washington University and edits poetry for Scablands Books. Find her on Twitter @MayaJZeller or visit her website: mayajewellzeller.com

ABOUT THE EDITORS

Andrew Shattuck McBride is a writer and editor based in Bellingham, Washington. His poem "I Was Happy as an Ant" was a semi-finalist for the 2017 *Crab Creek Review* Poetry Prize. Winner of a Walk Award in the Sue C. Boynton Poetry Contest, his work also appears in *Crab Creek Review, Pontoon Poetry, Mud Season Review, Connecticut River Review, So It Goes, Rise Up Review, Eclectica Magazine,* and in *Clover, A Literary Rag* as well as in anthologies including *Last Call* and *Noisy Water.* He edits novels, memoirs, poetry collections, and now—anthologies. @ASMcBride382

Jill McCabe Johnson is grateful to live on traditional Coast Salish lands. Books include *Revolutions We'd Hoped We'd Outgrown,* shortlisted for the Clara Johnson Award in Women's Literature, *Diary of the One Swelling Sea,* winner of a Nautilus Award in Poetry, poetry chapbook *Pendulum,* shortlisted for the Rane Arroyo Award, and nonfiction chapbook *Borderlines.* Honors include grants and fellowships from Artist Trust, the National Endowment for the Humanities, Hedgebrook, Playa, and Brush Creek Foundation for the Arts. She earned her MFA in Creative Writing from Pacific Lutheran University and her Ph.D. in English from the University of Nebraska-Lincoln. jillmccabejohnson.com @jmcjohnson

ACKNOWLEDGEMENTS & NOTES

Luther Allen's "sinking" from *Refugium: Poems for the Pacific* (Caitlin, 2017).

James Bertolino's "Whales" published in *Snail River*, Quarterly Review of Literature Award Series, 1995.

Yvonne Blomer's "Our One Blue Bowl" published on the City of Victoria website and will appear as a piece of city art as part of Yvonne's legacy project as Victoria's Poet Laureate

Allen Braden's "Instructions on Being a Sea Creature" published by *Orion Magazine*, November/December, 2014.

Jennifer Bullis' "Claude Lévi-Strauss Paces the Beach at Point Whitehorn, Washington" published in *WA129*, edited by Tod Marshall (Sage Hill, 2017).

Christine Clarke's "Return to Salish Sea" was published as part of the City of Seattle's Poetry on Buses program.

Sarah DeWeerdt's "To these legacy chemicals" source: Desforges, J.P. *et al.* "Predicting global killer whale population collapse from PCB pollution." *Science* 361, 1373-1376, 2018.

An earlier version of Heather Durham's "Earth to Earth" appeared in *Blue Lyra Review*, Issue 5.3, Fall 2016.

Bob Friel's "Orcas in the Mist" published in *Outside Online*, August 27, 2018.

Sam Hamill's "The End of the Road from Nantucket" from *Habitation* (Lost Horse, 2014). Published with permission from the Sam Hamill Literary Estate.

Ernestine Saankaláxt Hayes' "Surrounded by Freedom" excerpted from *Blonde Indian* (Sun Tracks, 2006), is reprinted by permission of the University of Arizona Press. *Blonde Indian* was awarded the American Book Award.

Christopher Howell's "Meltdown" published in *The Bellingham Review*, Issue 63, 2011.

Jenifer Browne Lawrence's "Landscape with No Net Loss" published in *WA129*, edited by Tod Marshall (Sage Hill, 2017).

Mark Leiren-Young's "For the Honoured Dead" includes research available from The Center for Whale Research (whaleresearch.com) and Orca Net (orcanet.org).

Paula MacKay's "Dio" adapted from earlier publication in *Earth Island Journal*, October 25, 2018.

Tim McNulty's "Ascendance" from *Ascendance* (Pleasure Boat Studio, 2013).

David Mason's "Salmon Leap" from *Sea Salt* (Red Hen, 2014).

Christen Mattix's "Record Salmon Run" published in *Psaltery & Lyre*, Issue 104, October 23, 2014.

JM Miller's "Orca" from *Wilderness Lessons* (FutureCycle, 2016).

Jim Milstead's "Articulations" from *Collage* (Independent Writers' Studio, 2015).

Jed Myers' "Pull of the Moon" published in *Valparaiso Poetry Review*, Spring/Summer 2017: Volume XVIII, Number 2.

Cynthia Neely's "Inside Passage" from *Broken Water* (*Flyway: Journal of Writing and Environment*, 2011) and *Flight Path* (Aldrich, 2014).

Paul E. Nelson's "Elegy for Tahlequah's Calf" published in *Cascadia Magazine*, July 30, 2018.

Nancy Pagh's "Spring Salmon at Night" published in *No Sweeter Fat* (Autumn House, 2006).

Dayna Patterson's "Whale Watching" published by *A Mother Here: Art & Poetry Contest* (amotherhere.com), 2014.

Ronda Piszk Broatch's "Becoming Anadromous" from *Lake of Fallen Constellations* (MoonPath, 2015).

Diane Raptosh's "Dear Zygote" published in *Leviathan: A Journal of Melville Studies*, Volume 19, Number 3, October 2017.

Paisley Rekdal's "Ballard Locks" published in *Virginia Quarterly Review*, 86.2, Spring 2010.

Rachel Rose's "What We Heard About the Sea" published in *Song & Spectacle* (Harbour Publishing, 2012).

An earlier version of Adrienne Ross Scanlan's "Orcas in Passing" appeared in *Adventum Magazine*, Volume 1, Summer 2011.

Eva Saulitis' "Halfway Down an Alder Slope" and "In the Tlingit Language" from *Leaving Resurrection: Chronicles of a Whale Scientist* (Boreal Books, 2008), published with permission from the Eva Saulitis Literary Estate.

Tina Schumann's "Interlude" published in *Michigan Quarterly Review*, Issue 57.4, Fall 2017.

Betty Scott's "Central Healing" published in *Central Heating: Poems that Celebrate Love, Loss and Planet Earth* (Cave Moon, 2018).

Betty Scott's "Orcas Call" from *Writers' Corner Anthology 2018* (Chuckanut Editions, 2018).

Derek Sheffield's "Between Highway 2 and the Wenatchee" published in *Through the Second Skin* (Orchises, 2013).

Derek Sheffield's "Indivisible" from *Awake in the World* (Riverfeet, 2017).

Peggy Shumaker's "Sea Change" and "What to Count On" from *Underground Rivers* (Red Hen, 2002).

Ana Maria Spagna's "Another Strand" from *Reclaimers* (University of Washington, 2015).

Scott T. Starbuck's "Stranger" published in *Carbonfish Blues* (Fomite, 2018).

Ira Sukrungruang's "Dear Baby Bo" is an excerpt from "Letters in the Early Morning Light," published by *The Rumpus*.

Robert Sund's "In America" and "Salmon Moon" from *Poems From Ish River Country: Collected Poems and Translations* (Shoemaker & Hoard, 2004) used with permission by the Robert Sund Poet's House.

Ellen Welcker's "Weapon" published in *Pinwheel Journal*, Summer 2014.

Brooke Williams' "I Spot a Fin" excerpted from *Halflives: Reconciling Work and Wildness* (Johnson Books, 2003).

Carolyne Wright's "Triple Acrostic: Orcas" published in *Shake the Tree, Volume I* (Brightly, 2015).

Maya Jewell Zeller's "Black Plastic Night" published in *Pacifica Literary Review*, Issue 9, Winter 2017.

A special thank you to the National Endowment for the Humanities for their support for Jill McCabe Johnson, Ph.D., to participate in the NEH Summer Institute for College and University Teachers: The Native American West: A Case Study of the Columbia Plateau, led by co-directors Christopher Leise, Ph.D. and Laurie Arnold, Ph.D. (Colville).

CPSIA information can be obtained
at www.ICGtesting.com
Printed in the USA
LVHW040427291119
638727LV00025B/3492/P